A Shooting Anthology

A Shooting Anthology

Edited by
Michael Brander

SWAN·HILL
PRESS

Illustrations
The illustrations in the book are the work of Colin Woolf

Copyright © 1993 by Michael Brander (text)
Illustrations © 1993 Colin Woolf

First published in the UK in 1993
by Swan Hill Press
an imprint of Airlife Publishing Ltd

British Library Cataloguing in Publication Data
A catalogue record for this book
is available from the British Library

ISBN 1 85310 325 X

Printed by Livesey Ltd., Shrewsbury.

Swan Hill Press
an imprint of Airlife Publishing Ltd.
101 Longden Road, Shrewsbury SY3 9EB, England

The Art of Shooting Flying
and
Hunting through the Centuries with Rifle, Gun, Dog and Sow
An Anthology of Sporting Writing
From the Seventeenth Century To the Present Day

The Art of Shooting Flying

In 1644 Alonzo Martinez de Espinar, writing on shooting in Spain in his book *Arte de Ballesteria y Monteria,* recorded:

They [partridges] are shot with an arquebus flying, and for that reason do not exist in such numbers as formerly, nor are there any longer such pointing dogs to find them with cleverness so great that quantities of them could be killed with a crossbow. In those days the sportsmen were most dexterous and now such are wanting; for as the game is killed more easily, nobody wishes to waste his time in training dogs, as the man has not to shoot partridges on the ground; and the only use he has for dogs is to flush game and that takes no training as the dog does it naturally.

There seems to have been no shortage of partridges in France in 1666 when an entry for 21 March in Pepys' diary reads: Sir John Long told us of the plenty of partridges in France, where he says the King of France and his company killed with their guns in the plain of Versailles, 300 odd partridges at one bout. Whether this entry indicated a real or imagined shortage of partridges in Britain, it is noteworthy that in 1673 Charles II's French gamekeeper, M. Favennes de Mouchant requested permission to import some French partridges. The Marquis de Croissy, ambassador for Louis XIV to Charles II duly arranged for these first *Perdix rouges* to be sent from the park at Chambord.

Alonzo Martinez de Espinar's nostalgic comments were palpably false, since not only have large bags of partridges been regularly shot in Spain right up to the present day, but in the following century many fine Spanish pointers were imported into Britain and other parts of Europe. However, it does seem that the continent was once again well ahead of Britain, for the 'art of shooting flying' is not mentioned in Britain until 1686 in Richard Blome's compilation *The Gentleman's Recreation.* In this he noted:

It is now the Mode to shoot flying, as being by Experience found the best and surest way; for when your Game is on the wing, it is more exposed to Danger, for if but one shot hits any Part of the Wing so expanded, it will occasion its Fall, altho' not to kill it; so that your Spaniel will soon be its Victor, and, if well disciplined to the Sport, will bring it to you.

As well as demonstrating the degree of shooting proficiency attained at that date in Britain this passage explodes another of de Espinar's gloomy theories. The need for well-trained gundogs was, of course, as great as ever. At this stage the pointer seems to have been little known, or used, in Britain. Setters, used for netting and falconry, were principally used to find game in the open and spaniels bustled it up from cover. Both were probably expected to retrieve shot game and crossbow bolts, either from cover, or water, if necessary. Gundogs were still expected to be general purpose animals.

In 1671 Charles II's Restoration Parliament passed a game act which prohibited all freeholders of under one hundred pounds a year, or the vast majority of yeoman landowners from killing game, even on their own land. This piece of discriminatory legislation and its enforcement over the next 150 years was to cause more bitterness and ill-feeling amongst country people than almost any other government regulation. Furthermore it ensured that shooting as a sport became thoroughly unpopular in the countryside, especially since those who were 'qualified' by the act might shoot where they wished, unless warned off by the landowner, or his gamekeeper.

The best light fowling-pieces in the early part of the seventeenth century were of French or Italian manufacture. As the number of these guns imported into Britain began to increase, a great deal of rubbish found its way into the country. This was particularly the case about the time of the Restoration and the Gunmakers' Company was given powers to require guns to be submitted to proof before being sold; they were checked for safety by a much larger charge being fired through the barrels than was required, to ensure that they would withstand the normal charge without bursting. Guns so 'proofed' were stamped on the barrels with identifying marks.

According to Blome, the gun most suitable for shooting flying:

...should be about Four Feet and a half long in the Barrel and of a pretty wide Bore, something under a Musket. You should have your Gun always cock'd in Readiness with your thumb over the Cock, for fear of its going off contrary to your intention; so that when you meet with any Game you must be quick, and having got aim to your Mind let fly with all Expedition.

He went on to mention shooting from horseback and the need for control of the horse, adding:

Some are of the Opinion that you must shoot something before the Fowl otherwise it will be past before the Shot can come to it; but this is a vulgar Error, for no Game can fly so quick, but that the Shot will meet it; for the Shot flyeth as wide as about the Compass of a Bushel, if rightly order'd in the Charging. Yet I am of the Opinion if the Game flyeth as it were over your Head, that 'tis best to aim at the Head; and if it flyeth from you to aim as it were under its Belly. And 'tis found best to let the Game fly a little past you before you let fly, for thereby the Shot will better enter the Body.

In shooting, whether the Game be flying, or on the Ground, or a Tree or Hedge, always (as near as you can) endeavour to shoot with the wind and not against it and rather sideways or behind the Fowl than in their Faces and not at a single Fowl if you can compass more within your Level; and if on a Tree, Hedge, or on the Ground seek the convenientest shelter you can of Hedge, Bank, Tree, or the like to be absconded from the Fowl's seeing you, which is

very offensive to them; and being within shot and a fair Mark, lose not Time, but let Fly.

The first to write on shooting definitively in terms recognizable today was Colonel Peter Hawker in his authoritative work *Instructions to Young Sportsmen in all that relates to Guns and Shooting,* which was first published in 1816 and ran into eleven editions. The first to write entertainingly on shooting as a sport, however, was Colonel Thomas Thornton, a wealthy and eccentric all-round Yorkshire sportsman. Educated at Glasgow University, he was also a Francophil, and visited the Highlands to fish and shoot for a number of years between 1784 and 1800. He published a book in 1804 entitled *A Sporting Tour of the Northern Parts of England and Great Part of the Highlands of Scotland,* in which he described the shooting and fishing he enjoyed. This was the forerunner of many subsequent books and although marred here and there by occasional inaccuracies and somewhat boastful overtones, it provides a very entertaining picture of the sport to be had at the time. It is particularly worth noting that at this period he regarded double-barrelled guns as 'mere knick-knacks', although by the end of the eighteenth century they were in common use.

Here is Thomas Thornton's account of a day in the Cairngorms close to Aviemore around the year 1784:

August 6. At half past four we were awakened and a finer morning never ushered in the day. The whole house was roused, but it being the first excursion of the kind this season, many things were mislaid, though every precaution had been taken by me the evening before.

Started at eight, found the Spey unfordable and were obliged to ride round above four miles, by Ruthven Ferry. I ordered the servants, with two brace of pointers...to cross over in a boat and meet us on a hill marked out; and then, agreeing to make one of the gullies of snow our guide, we proceeded; but there being a valley full of corn and the river Fische to cross, were obliged to bend about a mile further than we expected, Up the vale of Fische is an extreme wild view; at ten o'clock we were at the foot of the mountain, the heat intense, the mercury standing at 84 Fahrenheit.

A severe labour we had to ascend this mountain, as steep as the side of a house; rocky and sometimes boggy; whilst frequently large stones, on which our horses stept with apparent security, would give way, and whirl down the precipice; so that they were frightened beyond imagination...At twelve o'clock we got up to the first snow, and, before one, we thought we were near the mouth of Glen Ennoch, and then depositing our Champaign, lime, shrub, porter, &c, in one of the large snow drifts, beneath an arch, from which ran a charming spring, we agreed to dine there. In my way up the pointers had found some game, and I killed at two points, an old moor cock and a ptarmigant, which I ordered to be well picked and prepared for dinner.

Having rested a few minutes, the gentlemen left their horses in the care of the servants...They then kept moving forward... and...at last arrived at the top.

10

It is impossible to describe the astonishment of the whole party when they perceived themselves on the brink of that frightful precipice, which separated them from the lake below!...Let the reader figure to himself a mountain at least eighteen thousand feet above him, and a steep precipice of thirteen thousand feet below, encompassed by conical and angular rocks...while the solemn silence, interrupted only by the hoarse notes of the ptarmigants, increasing at the approach of strangers, or by the dashing of the never-ceasing cascades, soothes the mind with the most agreeable emotions.

[The rest of the party went on down to the lake leaving Thornton behind] In the interval I attempted to kill a ptarmigant or two, simply to pass the time, not being desirous of risking my leg much, and occasionally looking for my friends, whom I imagined I saw, but found afterwards that I was deceived by the distance.

After five hours absence, they came up, quite exhausted, and found me looking for some ptarmigants I had killed, as specimens for Mr Garrard (the artist attached to the party), but, unwilling to load myself on so hot a day, I had collected and left them near where I had shot them, and now anxiously sought for them near two hours without success. At length by the assistance of Dargo, they were found. Captain Waller had begged me to leave him to himself till he recovered, he was so much fatigued.

A thought struck me; I placed a ptarmigant, in such a position, that it appeared to be alive, and then mentioning to the captain that I had seen one, which he never had. Immediately on discovering it, he fired and shot it; this revived him more than any thing I could have given him. The having shot a ptarmigant was now the only topic of his conversation, and it would have been cruel to have undeceived him.

Our dinner, which was soon dressed, proved an excellent one; the chief dish consisted of two brace and a half of ptarmigants and a moor cock, a quarter of a pound of butter, some slices of Yorkshire-smoked ham, and rein-deer's tongue; with some sweet herbs, pepper &c prepared by the housekeeper at Raits. These with a due proportion of water, made each of us a plate of very strong soup, which was relished with a keenness of appetite that none but those who have been at Glen Ennoch can experience...

As is plain from this account Thornton could not always be relied on for accuracy, but the Highlanders at this time also had something of a reputation for unreliability. The following extracts from Thornton's diary are contrasted with extracts from Aeneas Mackintosh of Moy's diary covering the same period and the same events, during the time Colonel Thornton was staying with him as his guest. The first entry is from Thornton's diary:

October 4 — Morning most heavenly and the country perfectly dry...The carriage being obliged to wait for some iron work mending could not leave Aviemore till past three o'clock...Mr Garrard and I proceeded in the gig. The road from hence to Moy, where we were engaged to dine is tolerable...As our

11

horses were fresh and we intended resting them a day or two at Moy, we went at a pretty good rate...About half a mile from Moy, the spring of the carriage, not being sufficiently mended gave way and we got out and walked along the loch, ordering our horses out...Got to Moy about eight o'clock and found the laird politely ready to receive us...

Aeneas Mackintosh of Moy does not even match Thornton's dates, but as the latter had compressed several journeys into one it is likely that Mackintosh is the more accurate at least in this respect. He wrote:

22nd September; Return to Moy about half past seven in the evening. Colonel Thornton an English Squire from Yorkshire, arrives in company with Mr Garret, a landscape painter, after I had given over all hopes of seeing him, though they had promised to be with me this night on the 15 at Aviemore.

Thornton's account then neatly compresses two days into one and continues:

Day continued showery until eleven, when I sallied out, accompanied by the laird, who, though no sportsman, was polite enough to show me the likeliest ground for black game, by which act of civility he was more than once in danger of a fall; for, being mounted on an English gelding, not at all accustomed to wild, moory ground, he found it no easy matter to follow my horses, real Highlanders, perpetually trained to the business.

We found plenty of black game and some moor-game, both of which, owing to the rain, were exceedingly wild. The black game would not allow me to come near them, except in birch-cover, so thick that it was almost impossible to get a shot. With great labour, however, I killed five, but lost one, which I saw fall near a stream, and suppose it must have floated down.

After taking a great deal of pains to no purpose, I returned home...Got quickly dressed, and sat down to an excellent dinner...Returns; black-game five.

Sir Aeneas saw the day rather differently, noting by total contrast:

23rd Sept. The Colonel goes a-shooting. Out of compliment I attend him on horseback through a rough moor to the West of the house covered with birch wood and shrubs. See from a dozen to fifteen black game, of which he kills one, but by four, being tired and my leg very uneasy, return and obliged to wait dinner till seven in the evening.

The next day Thomas Thornton, blissfully unaware of his host's growing irritation with his southern visitors, wrote:

October 5 — Morning delightful. The laird's family do not rise with the lark but take a comfortable nap; I therefore amused myself by ordering the nets to be cast into the lake to try for some char, and we caught a few, very fine; from one of which Mr Garrard made a beautiful drawing...

I now adjusted my bullet gun, by which time the company came downstairs; and at twelve I went out, intending to try for a roebuck, which were said to be more plentiful and better preserved on this estate than in any part of Scotland.

I confess my patience had been so much tried before, that, though I proceeded, I thought my prospect of success very small; but I took all imaginable pains, and saw one, or a brace; yet they were so deep in cover, and sprang so quick, that my eye could scarce follow them...took one cast more, and got the glimpse of another, at which I shot, and seeing one bound from the place, feared he was only slightly wounded; when coming up to the rocky, but bushy, ground he was on, found him dead, being shot through the heart, and ordered the Highlander, who was with me, to take him home, after I had thoroughly examined him...Returned to the mansion, where the laird added much to the satisfaction my success had given me, by the pleasure it seemed to afford him.

Returns of the day; shot a roebuck and four moor-game...

Sir Aeneas's entry could scarcely be a greater contrast in every way. He wrote scathingly:

24th Sept. The Colonel having applied for leave to shoot a roebuck, send my servant to attend him, and go myself to visit my farms in the neighbourhood, which I frequently do. Return by four when I understand that Thornton had killed a doe giving suck. I in consequence entertain him very coolly and form in my mind that it was the first and the last he should kill any time he should be at my house. My observations on the subject to be enlarged.

Thornton, apparently still continuing unaware of his host's extremely poor opinion of his sporting activities, appears to have kept Sir Aeneas up late and compounded the error by then leaving early, with the roe deer, whether buck or doe.

Thornton wrote:

October 6 — Morning very rainy, which prevented me taking a ride I had promised myself before I proceeded to Inverness...the road...over the most dreary, barren country...The inn we put up at is a modern building...Mr G. to whom I sent the roebuck...having made a very accurate drawing, had prudently, ordered a pasty and haunch for dinner...'

Sir Aeneas, no doubt gnashing his teeth with rage, wrote:

Sept 25th. From irregular hours and my chagrin at Thornton's behaviour obliged to lie in bed longer than usual. Thornton goes to Inverness and carries the doe with him. Yorkshire huntsmen, observations thereon. The Colonel makes present of the deer at Inverness instead of leaving him with me.

Just who was embroidering the truth and why is a matter for conjecture, but it is perhaps significant that on the subject of the deer it was Sir Aeneas who seemed to have its sex muddled at times. Thornton was an early riser and heavy drinker, also a hard-driving sportsman. Aeneas Mackintosh was used to late nights and to heavy drinking, so that his complaints on this score sound like sanctimonious humbug. It was ever the Highland attitude to be extremely hospitable to a guest, whatever might have been thought of him in reality.

Thornton, by his own account, does not seem to have been much of a deer-stalker, even so he could hardly mistake the sex of the animal. If he accidentally shot a doe out of season, however, it is not out of the question that for the purposes of his records he might have brazenly changed its sex. Aeneas Mackintosh really had no obvious reason to depart from the truth, although his obvious chagrin at not being presented with the venison for his own table perhaps might have prejudiced his account.

In those days there was no hard and fast close season and although it could have been a late fawn, it was rather far on in the season for a doe to be suckling young even in the Highlands, whether the date was early October or the end of September. The probability in any event is that the fawn was by then well enough grown to be perfectly capable of surviving on its own. This is a point Aeneas Mackintosh should have known perfectly well, even if he was obviously no sort of sportsman, so that the question of who was being economical with the truth remains open.

Thornton appears to have suffered from the common failure of British sportsmen, accustomed to shooting small birds, namely an inability to kill larger moving targets such as deer, probably due to inexperience, or buck-fever, or a combination of the two. It is interesting that this failure on the part of many good English shots was noted in North America around the turn of the eighteenth century by a Major Hazzard of Beaufort, South Carolina. Describing a typical Carolina hunting party around 1800 he wrote:

...the largest portion of our country is one continuous forest, interspersed throughout which...there are a great number of swamps...their width vary from half a mile to three, they are thick covers and therefore complete shelter for all kinds of our game, which are always to be found more or less in them. A day being fixed upon for a general hunt all the sportsmen meet at a given point with their huntsmen and hounds, there are few of us who keep more than ten couple, but then everyone having some dogs they make a very large pack, when they are all collected; the sportsmen are then equally divided, one half going one side of the swamp and the other part on the opposite side; they then arrange themselves within gunshot of each other and being all armed with double-barrel guns, are ready for the sport, which commences the moment the dogs and huntsmen are turned in; these swamps are skirted with very fine high pine barrens, which being open are famous shooting ground; soon as the dogs enter, the game run out, and are fired upon by the first sportsmen they come to, they then take back to cover and double with the dogs in full cry. It is not unusual in one of the largest swamps to drive out of them in one day's hunt deer, wolves, bears, foxes, wild cats and a great quantity of wild turkeys, and of which the sportsmen shoots as he thinks proper. We never follow one deer after he has made his escape out of the swamp unless he is wounded, for there is no running down deer with us; there being so many dogs, if suffered to pursue far, would soon be divided into a number of packs, but our wolf we always run down and as they are very strong and large they will run for three to four or five hours, if they are not shot in the chase, they come to bay in a thick cover and always turn their backs to a hurricane root [a tree blown down by the wind] where they will defend themselves against the largest pack, their bite being very severe. Our bears, foxes and wild cats are soon tired, when they always take to trees from which they are shook down to the dogs. The sportsmen particularly admire that part of the diversion, the shooting of our wild turkeys, which fly out of the swamps, whilst our dogs are in chase. They are very large and fly with great velocity and are very fine eating. It is remarkable that the English gentlemen who hunt frequently with us shoot very badly at our large game and yet will kill the smaller sorts with the greatest ease. I have known a gentleman shoot on the wing any of our fleet flying birds without missing a shot, and yet miss five, six and seven shots at deer and turkey in a day. I attribute this to agitation occasioned by the velocity with which they pass and their not being accustomed to them. I have in one day's hunt seen started forty deer and ten killed besides a number of other game; the spoils after the hunt is over, which is at dark, are equally divided among all the sportsmen, when the huntsmen set off with their respective hounds and all the sportsmen with the strangers are invited to dine at one of the sportsmen's seats, where a general dinner is always provided and which the whole alternatively find.

Colonel Thomas Thornton was one of the leading sportsmen of his day, falconer, fox-hunter and shot, as well as a considerable athlete. In 1794 he published a pamphlet entitled 'An Elucidation of a Mutinous Conspiracy Entered into by the Officers of the West York Militia against their Commanding officer: dedicated Sans Permission to H.R.H.Duke of York'. In this Thornton claimed that because he had exposed the Duke cheating at cards the latter had arranged for him to be court-martialled on false evidence. This was tilting at the Establishment with a vengeance. Colonel George Hangar, by contrast was one of the Prince Regent's inner circle of toadies, but his book *To All Sportsmen* written in 1814 contained some strange theories on dealing with poachers.

In those days poaching was still a very serious offence punishable by transportation. With many unemployed ex-soldiers returned from the wars on the continent and accustomed to living off the land, battles between armed poachers and gamekeepers could be desperate affairs at times. Colonel George Hangar's method of preventing poaching in a game preserve was clearly entirely theoretical, for had it ever been put into practice it would no doubt have scared off any would-be poachers, but what it would have done to the game is a point he does not seem to have considered. He wrote:

...had I a manor, and my house lay close to my preserve cover...I would...plant a six-pounder cannon on a platform at the top of the house [close to the preserve] thus loaded; Buy a bushel of marbles, such as the boys play with... put a double-handful into the cannon; and have clay balls, just the size of the calibre of the gun, made and baked at the clay-kilns, first boring three or four holes with an iron, nearly as big as your little finger, through and through them. This ball, when fired from the cannon, will make a most terrible whizzing noise, and together with the marbles buzzing about a fellow's ears, would make him think the very devil was in the wood. I would also build my

gamekeeper a house on one flank on the opposite side of the wood, with no door nor window below. The lower rooms might be easily lighted from above; and the door ten feet up from the ground. He might draw the ladder up at night.

In this castle he might stand a siege, for it would be impossible to set fire to the house. And a round tower of about thirty feet, like the martello towers, only in miniature, with a six-pounder mounted at the top of it, with a door going out from the corner of his bed-room up to the platform on which the cannon is planted, should also be built. Thus either the gamekeeper, or I, should from our positions, always have a flanking fire on the enemy. I am of the opinion, if, about two or three times a week, my gamekeeper and self were to fire about three or four rounds each, into the wood, that the very devil himself would not go into it, when he once knew that such manoeuvres therein were frequently practiced; that is to say after it was dark. I do not think, if I may judge by my own feeling, that it would either be pleasant or prudent. My motive for firing the cannon with a baked clay-ball, is, that an iron ball would damage the timber; so would iron grape-shot; but marbles will not...

Although he may have seen action in America and Europe, George Hangar clearly knew next to nothing of sport in his native country.

Colonel Thornton, a strong Francophil, took advantage of the short Peace of Amiens in 1802 to travel to France for a sporting tour in a specially adapted coach, with an extensive armoury, his current mistress, an accompanying artist, pointers and a pack of hounds. He presented Napoleon with a brace of pistols and enjoyed some interesting sport as this account of shooting near Orléans on 20 August demonstrates:

I rose early next morning for the purpose of shooting with M. Belanger in the home park, to the south east of the Castle [belonging to M. de Lucays] This consists of about four thousand acres, inclosed within a stone wall...The scenery was so enchanting that I really attended to it more for the sake of Mr Bryant's pencil [his accompanying artist], than for the diversion of shooting. However the terriers were thrown in, and I shot two brace and a half of partridges. I then quitted Home Close and near the castle, in a fallow, half covered with thistles, the dogs drew, and stood, when a covey immediately rose of three brace and a half. I killed a bird with each barrel and marked another brace, which I also roused and killed, but took particular care not to shoot at the old birds.

Having hunted in the dogs, we saw seven or eight brace of quails; got two random shots and three points and killed them. A leveret also happened to come near me, which I shot at and she fell after running a few yards. The dogs flushed several other coveys, most of which were red-legged; but as the morning became very warm, and I heard the sound of the breakfast bell, I bagged seven brace of partridges, two brace and a half of quail, and the leveret, and giving my gun to the keeper returned to breakfast.

...The ladies were all delighted with my success and I must do this amiable family the justice to say, they were evidently anxious that I should enjoy all sorts of sporting in the highest perfection.

After our repast I went on horseback to inspect some forests of two and three hundred acres, lying to the south-east of the castle. I took my pointer with me, and the keeper carried my gun. In some grass I perceived that the dog drew, and at last stood. I therefore went up to him, when a covey of red-legged partridges rose, but all dispersed, by degrees, one or a brace at a time. I brought down one brace, but thought them too small and too near the house, to kill any more. However, as I had marked several on an adjoining piece of oats, I tried my dog and he behaved so as to astonish the keeper.

Having re-mounted, I rode through a small, but beautiful forest, cut into rides and abounding with rivulets. Here I understood were abundance of woodcocks, with some roebucks and foxes; and in an adjoining forest, plenty of wild-boars. I here remarked a greater profusion of heath than I had previously seen in any part of France.

Just as we entered the second forest I saw a bird of a very singular appearance fly along, and attempted to get a shot at it, but could not. The keeper did not know its name. This forest is admirably adapted for wild-boars, being remarkably thick and swampy; but on looking at my watch, I found the time had passed so rapidly I was compelled to think of returning.

A brace of barren birds, which were basking close to the road, rose at my approach, and alighted in some corn, where I killed them. The keeper at the same time observed a covey alight about two hundred yards distant, and I immediately killed a brace and a half, all of which were strong half-grown birds.

The horses were so dreadfully tormented by flies, that a fine blood mare, rode by the keeper, taking fright at the report of my gun, turned short round, and plunged at me, but fortunately missing her aim, she only struck the stock of my gun, which was forced with such violence against the cap of my knee, that I really thought at first it had broken the bone. However, as the dog was still standing, I hobbled up to him, and killed an old grey partridge. We then returned to the castle, which we did not reach till near seven o'clock...

Thornton went on to enjoy some good sport in the extensive estate of the Château de Chambord. After Waterloo, when peace in Europe was established at last, he left England to take up domicile in France and rented the palatial château and sporting estate from the widow of Napoleon's Marshal Berthier, who had been created Prince of Wagram. In typically Napoleonic manner his widow was left without a pension. She was no doubt glad to lease the vast château and estate in 1817 to the eccentric English sportsman, although he stabled his horses in one of the principal (then ruined) salons. He also took a delight in styling himself Duc de Chambord, both of which facts are conveniently ignored in most modern French guide-books of the château.

After leasing the Château de Chambord he subsequently bought an estate at Pont-sur-Seine, which carried with it the title of Marquis. He then occasionally styled himself Marquis du Pont to poke fun at the British aristocracy. Thornton eventually retired to Paris. There he formed a Falconer's Club at which he dined regularly. He died in 1823 having ordered his hounds out and with his horse waiting at the door.

By the turn of the eighteenth century the standard of shooting dogs, especially of pointers and setters, seems to have been very poor, although no doubt then as now it varied in different parts of the country. In the south of England near the New Forest area it seems to have been particularly low as this interesting account extracted from *Rural Sports* (1801) by the Revd William Barker Daniel on the training of a sow to point demonstrates:

Toomer [formerly one of the King's Keepers in the New Forest and afterwards gamekeeper to Sir Henry Mildmay] actually broke a black sow to find Game, and to back and stand; and SLUT was as staunch as any Pointer...Slut was bred in, and was of that sort which maintain themselves in the New Forest without regular feeding, except when they have young, and then but for a few Weeks, and was given, when about three months old, to be a Breeding Sow, by Mr Thomas to Mr Richard Toomer, both at that time Keepers in the Forest. From having no young she was not fed, or taken very little notice of, until about eighteen months old, was seldom observed near the Lodge, but chanced to be seen one day when Mr Edward Toomer was there. The Brothers were concerned together in breaking Pointers and Setters, some of their own breeding, and others which were sent to be broke by different Gentlemen; of the latter, although they would *stand* and *back,* many were so indifferent, that they would neither *hunt* nor express any Satisfaction when Birds were killed and put before them. This slackness in these Dogs first suggested the Idea, that by the same Method any other Animal might be made to *stand* and do as well as one of these huntless and inactive Pointers. At this instant the Sow passed by, and was remarked as being extremely handsome; R.Toomer threw her a piece or two of Oatmeal Roll, for which she appeared grateful, and approached very near; from that time they were determined to make a *Sporting Pig* of her. The first step was to give her a *Name* and that of SLUT (given in consequence of her soiling herself in a Bog) she acknowledged in the course of the Day and never afterwards forgot. Within a *Fortnight* she would find and point *Partridges* or *Rabbits,* and her training was much forwarded by the abundance of both which were near the Lodge; she daily improved, and in a few Weeks would RETRIEVE birds that had ran, as well as the best Pointer; nay, her Nose was superior to any Pointer they ever possessed, and no two Men in England had better. They hunted her principally on the Moors and Heaths. SLUT has stood *Partridges, Black-game, Pheasants,*

Snipes and *Rabbits* in the same Day, but was never known to point a HARE.
She was seldom taken by choice more than a mile or two from the Lodge, but
has frequently joined them when out with their Pointers, and continued with
them several Hours. She has sometimes stood a *Jack-Snipe* when all the
Pointers had passed by it; she would *back* the Dogs when they pointed, but the
Dogs refused to back her until spoke to, their Dogs being all trained to make a
general *halt* when the Word was given, whether any Dog pointed or not; so
that she has been frequently standing in the midst of a Field of Pointers. In
consequence of the Dogs not liking to hunt when she was with them (for they
dropped their Sterns and shewed Symptoms of Jealousy) she did not very often
accompany them, except for the Novelty; or when she accidentally joined them
in the Forest. Her pace was mostly a TROT, was seldom known to *Gallop,*
except when called to go out Shooting, she would then come home off the
Forest at full Stretch, (for she was never shut up, but to prevent her being out
of the sound of the *call* or *whistle,* when a party of Gentlemen has appointed to
see her out the next day, and which Call she obeyed as readily as a Dog) and
be as much elevated as a Dog upon being shewn the Gun. She always
expressed great pleasure when Game, either dead or alive, was placed before
her. She has frequently stood a single Partridge at *forty yards* distance, her
Nose in a direct line to the Bird; after *standing* some considerable time, she

21

would *drop* like a *Setter,* still keeping her Nose in an exact Line, and she would continue in that Position until the Game moved; if it took wing she would come up the place and put her Nose down two or three times; but if a Bird ran off, she would get up and go the place and draw slowly after it, and when the Bird stopped she would stand it as before. The two Mr TOOMERs lived about seven miles apart at *Rhinefield* and *Broomy* Lodges; SLUT has many times gone by herself from the one Lodge to the other, as if to court being taken out Shooting. She was about five years old when her Master died, and at the Auction of his Pointers &c., was included in the Sale, and bought in at *Ten Guineas,* Sir H. Mildmay having expressed a wish to have her, she was sent to Dogmersfield Park, where she remained several years; she was last in the possession of Col. SIKES, and was then *Ten years* old, and had become fat and slothful, but would point Game as well as before. When killed, which was at Bassilden House, SLUT weighed *seven hundred pounds;* her Death, to those who possess common feelings of Humanity, appears (if one may use the Expression) at least *Animal Murder;* it would have cost but a trifling Sum to have fed and sheltered her in the Winter and the Park would have supplied her Wants during the Summer at no Expense.

The following satirical account of six city tailor's apprentices' sporting activities with their guns and a fox-dog, a terrier, a Newfoundland bitch and a mastiff, in the vicinity of the City of London is an interesting period piece, extracted from *Sportascrapiana,* dated around 1800.

September 1st. — According to our agreement made at the Hole-in-the-Wall, six of us met on Blackfriar's bridge, at half-past five o'clock, armed, and furnished with a large supply of ammunition.

Squibb'd our guns over the bridge and got a volley of oaths from a west country barge that was passing under the centre arch.

Loaded and primed; gave the dogs a bit of bread each — the fox dog would not eat his — took a dram apiece, and set forward in high spirits, for the Circus Gate, on our way to Camberwell, where we were informed we would find several covies.

Just at Christ Church, Blackfriars, Ned Simple shot at a rat, and missed it; but it gave us a fine hunt, the dogs barking all the way, until we drove it into the Thames.

Beat over all the ground about the Halfpenny-hatches, and found nothing but one cat, which all of us fired at; but being only six in number, and a cat having nine lives, we missed killing, though we severely wounded her.

Passing at the back of Webber Row, we saw several pigeons; but though they were within pistol-shot, they flew so fast that none of us could take aim, although our guns were already cocked and loaded with No.2 six fingers deep.

Saw five sparrows on the ground opposite the Elephant and Castle, Newington, feasting on some new dropped horse dung — stole up with great caution within four yards of the game, and gave an irregular fire; but Bob Tape's musket going off before he took aim, the birds, we suppose, made their escape antecedent to the other five going off; for the devil a sparrow we killed.

Rather out of humour with such ill-luck — so took another dram a-piece and pushed briskly forward to Camberwell.

Met two men driving geese at Kennington Common — offered them eighteen-pence, which they accepted, for a shot at the flock at twenty yards. Drew lots for who should fire first. It fell to Billy Candlewick's chance, who, from his father belonging for many years to the Orange Regiment of the City Militia, knew something of taking aim.

The goose-driver stepped the ground, and Billy took aim for about ten minutes, when shutting both eyes, lest the pan might flash in his sight, he snapped and missed fire — he took aim a second time, snapped and missed again — borrowed Bob Tape's scissors, and hammered the flint — snapped and missed fire a third time — thought the devil had got hold of the gun, examined her, and found she was neither loaded nor primed. The goose-driver refused to let Billy try again, so we gave him another sixpence and he sold us a lame gander, which we placed at about six yards, and taking a shot a-piece, killed him, and put him in Ned Thimble's cabbage-net.

When we came within sight of the Swan, at Stockwell, we all ran as fast as we could, to see who should get in first, as we had settled to breakfast there. Unfortunately our guns being cocked, I made a stumble and the trigger being touched by something, off went the piece and lodged the contents in the body of a sucking pig that was crossing the road. The squeaking of the poor little animal roused the maternal affection of the sow, and set the fox dog, the terrier, the Newfoundland bitch, and the mastiff, a barking. The noise of the sow, the pig and the dogs, with the report of the gun, brought out the people of the house, and indeed of the neighbourhood, and being threatened by one, and laughed at by another, we thought it best to buy the pig at four shillings, which we did, and having put it into Bob Tape's game-bag, which, bye-the-bye, was nothing but a half a bolster tick, we made the best of our way to the Plough at Clapham, where we had some cold buttock and ale for breakfast.

Tried all the common round — Beat every bush with the muzzle of our guns, set the dogs in the pigs, and found but one chaffinch, which was rather wild, not letting us come within eight yards, so that we could not be sure of our bird. We hunted him from spray to spray for above an hour, without being able to get in a parallel line, so as to take sure aim, when at last he was killed by a little boy with a stone — bought him and put him into the net with the goose.

Resolved to make for Blackheath, and to cut across the country, that we might get amongst the stubbles — missed our road and by some kind of circumbendibus, got into Brixton Causeway, where we asked if there were any birds in the neighbourhood. We were directed to a dead horse, where two ravens and several magpies were assembled; but they would not stay our arrival, for the moment they saw us they made off.

Our pig-carrying companion and our goose-carrier complained of the weight, so we took charge of the game by turns.

Hunted a weasel for above an hour and lost him. The terrier was remarkably staunch.

Crossing a field near Camberwell, we thought we saw a covey of partridges at the side of a ditch — so we all made up to them with our guns cocked, tying the dogs to our legs, so that they might not run in and spring the game.

What we thought to be a covey of partridges proved to be a gang of gypsies, who were squatted down under the hedge, peeling turnips and preparing potatoes for dinner. It was the mercy of God we did not fire at them as all our pieces were up to our shoulders, and we had but one eye a-piece open, when that which we took to be the old cock rose up, and said in a loud voice, 'What the devil are you about?'

After much difficulties, and but little sport, got by the direction of the gypsies into Greenwich Road, where, being rather fatigued, we stopped at the Half-Way house until a coach came by, when mounting the roof and the box, we were conveyed near Blackheath, to our unspeakable joy.

Never saw the heath before — amazed at the number of furze bushes, and the wide extent there is for game. Had an excellent chase after a jackass, which the mastiff tore in the leg. Kept close together for fear of losing each other

Got down near a large round house — shot at a flock of sparrows, and killed one, which we think is a cock, his head being rather black.

Saw several brother sportsmen out, who had killed nothing but a hedge-hog and a tame jack-daw, which belonged to a public-house at New Cross Turnpike.

Got up to the main road — fired at a yellow-hammer, and frightened the horses in the Dover Stage. The guard threatened to shoot us, and we took to out heels.

Saw some black game flying very high. They looked for all the world like crows.

The terrier came to point at a thick bunch of fern. We were now sure this must be a covey of partridges and we prepared accordingly. The mastiff ran in and brought out one of the young ones. It proved to be a nest of field mice — took every one and put them into the bolster — Grass mice were better than nothing.

Much fatigued, and agreed to shoot all the way home — fired off our guns at the foot of Greenwich Hill, and were laughed at by the inhabitants — loaded them again and fired at a sheet of paper for half a hour, without putting a grain into it — got to Smith's at dusk, and discharged our pieces in the air before we went in — had something to eat and drink, then set off for the city, and squibbed our guns all the way, as long as the powder lasted.

Got home much fatigued with the day's sport — went to our club and told a thousand lies about the birds we killed, and the presents we made of them — smoked our pipes and by twelve got to bed.

Colonel Peter Hawker (1786–1853) is probably one of the best known sportsman of the early nineteenth century, both through his diaries and his book *Instructions to Young Sportsmen in all that relates to Guns and Shooting.* His diaries were edited initially in 1893 by Sir Ralph Payne-Gallwey and in 1931 by Eric Parker, a notable editor of *The Field* in his day. Eric Parker expressed surprise at the liberties that Payne-Gallwey had taken with the diary entries, but was not beyond altering them occasionally himself. The originals today are in the Yale Library, but the following extracts have been taken from photocopies of them. In 1808 Ensign Peter Hawker was stationed at Ipswich with his regiment prior to going to fight in the Peninsular Campaign. He wrote:

October 3rd. Went from Ipswich with a party amounting to near twenty, besides markers and beaters, to storm a preserved cover belonging to a Parson Bond, because he never allowed anyone a day's shooting, and had man-traps and dog gins all over his wood. I had made out a regular plan of attack and line of march, but our precision was frustrated by the first man we saw on reaching the ground, who was the keeper; we therefore had no time to hold a council of war, but rushed into cover like a pack of foxhounds before his face. Away he went, naming everyone he could, and we all joined him in the hue and cry of 'Where is Parson Bond?'

In the meantime our *feu de joie* was going on most rapidly. At last up came the parson, almost choked with rage. The two first people he warned off were Colonel Hawker and myself; having been served with notices we kept him in tow, while the others rallied his covers and serenaded him with an incessant bombardment in every direction. The confused rector did not know which way to run. The scene of confusion was ridiculous beyond anything, and the invasion of an army could scarce exceed the noise. Not a word could be heard for the cries of 'Mark!' 'Dead!' and 'Well done!' interspersed every moment with bang, bang and the yelping of barrack curs. The parson at last mustered his whole establishment to act as patriots against the marauders, footboys running one way, ploughmen mounted on carthorses, galloping the other, and everyone from the village that could be mustered was collected to repel the mighty shock. At last we retreated and about half-past four those who had escaped being entered in his domesday book renewed the attack. The parson having eased himself with a vomit began to speak more coherently and addressed himself to those, who being liable to an action for trespass, were obliged to stand in the footpath and take the birds as they flew over; at last so many were caught that the battle ceased. Though a large number of pheasants were destroyed the chase did not end in such aggregate slaughter as we expected, and not more than one third of those brought down were bagged in consequence of our being afraid to turn off our best dogs; we brought away some of the parson's traps, one of which was a most terrific engine and now hangs in the mess-room for public exhibition. Only one dog was caught all day and whose should that be but Parson Bond's! After leaving the covert I killed 2 partridges and 1 hare.

His diaries shed considerable light on the sporting life of the early nineteenth century. For instance his description of a stage-coach journey to Exeter in 1811 makes surprising reading today:

January 7th. At four in the morning got into the mail and at eleven at night reached Exeter. We were a delightfully jolly party, and not being a post day, the mail stopped whenever we saw game, and during the journey I killed four brace of partridges. When it was too dark to shoot, our party mounted the roof and sang choruses (which I joined in and drove) and in which the guard and coachman took a very able part.

In July 1816, after a visit to his friend Mr Rising, of Horsey in East Norfolk, he wrote:

July 15th. Came up from Norwich by way of Newmarket (110 miles) within 13 hours!! by the Light Telegraph morning coach, which beat the mail by nearly five hours.

N.B. Our object in going to Norfolk was to shoot young wildfowl...etc., but as the custom of that country is to sport in large *battue* parties, I at last gave up attempting to reckon what I killed myself, though I had far more sport than the others...the wildfowl shooting was most capital. We killed immense numbers of almost every kind of sea and marsh birds, interspersed with occasional good shooting at leverets and rabbits, young snipes, plovers, etc. The only birds however that I had not killed before were the Crested Grebes and Shoveller ducks, with which I had (one day in particular) most excellent sport. The circumstances that make the birds so plentiful here cancels all the pleasure in shooting which is — that the fear of death deters strangers from hazarding their constitution in such a pestilential climate! I came home unwell but was happy to escape as well as I did.

Although undeniably a considerable sportsman, Hawker was also an astonishing hypochondriac at times, but he provides a good picture of sport in his diaries. He was very friendly with Joseph Manton, the famous gunmaker, and studied all aspects of gunmaking, mastering most of them himself. His great delight was wildfowling, then almost unheard of as a gentleman's sport.

With the introduction of the percussion cap in 1818 shooting was to grow swiftly in effectiveness. Hitherto with the old flintlock guns one misfire in three shots had been about average. The new caps led to the introduction of the pin-fire action and finally to the breech-loader. Inevitably the change was resisted at first, even by such enthusiasts as Hawker himself, although later he handsomely acknowledged his own error.

The end result of this innovation, of course, was larger bags. Although admittedly some very remarkable bags had been made with flintlock guns, the really large bags, which ensued towards the end of the century would have been a physical impossibility with them. The bag produced by a royal duke for a day's partridge shooting in 1811 was, however, by no means typical. It read as follows:

Killed of Game	0
Wounded in legs	1 Marker slightly
Wounded in face	1 Groom severely
Wounded on head	1 Hat of friend
Ditto left rump	1 Horse

As the above extract illustrates this was a time of cruel social injustice, but hardly surprisingly one sees little of this in Hawker's diaries. Being a qualified person under the Game Act (of 1671) he was entitled to shoot over the land of complete strangers unless warned off either by the owner or his gamekeeper. Hawker, as we have seen, frequently boasted of doing this and even at times running away to avoid being warned off, so that he could return on another occasion. This was nothing but licensed poaching, yet in 1817 unarmed poaching by night was made punishable with seven years' transportation to Botany Bay. With the end of the Napoleonic Wars and the post-war slump, men would risk much rather than see their families starve. Even spring guns and mantraps would not deter them. If challenged at night armed gangs thought little of murdering the gamekeeper to avoid being caught.

There is hardly any mention of this in Hawker's diaries, but the steady speeding up of communications is very noticeable and ultimately this was to affect sport in Britain and elsewhere as much as almost any other factor. As the canals gave way to coaches and as the coaches increased their speeds on the fine new turnpike roads, eventually giving way to the railroads, not only was fresh country opened up to the sportsman, but game could be sent considerably greater distances, remaining fresh.

A contemporary of Hawker's, who was no sort of military man, but every sort of a sportsman, was Squire George Osbaldeston, a first-rate shot, a fine athlete and also one of the leading foxhunters of his day. Also born in 1786 his memoirs spanned nearly eighty years and included memories of many outstanding characters during the early years of the century when the Regency bucks and late Georgian sportsmen were particularly notable for their sporting feats and wagers, as well as their eccentricity. It is scarcely surprising that shooting standards sometimes left a great deal to be desired but perhaps because he normally shot only with first-rate shots Osbaldeston only recalled two near misses. His example of eccentric behaviour, however, is hard to beat. He wrote:

A guest of mine once gave me a good fright while shooting in Yorkshire. He was a very good and generally a careful shot; but on this occasion he lapsed from his usual discretion. I was exceedingly lame at the time, and having no shooting pony, I shot off a donkey who stood fire like an artilleryman. My friend was walking a short distance before me when some partridges flew up, he turned and levelled at a bird which was flying in a direct line for my face. A donkey is not a very nimble animal, at least you cannot make him move very quickly, and I thought my last moment had come. I was not much reassured when, in answer to my shout to take care what he was doing, my friend answered; 'Oh, I saw you at the end of my gun. There is no danger.' It did not occur to him, apparently, that when a man has his finger on the trigger and is intent on a partridge, he may fire before he realises that there is another victim a little further away than the bird. I was not more than 15 or 16 yards from him.

I was much less fortunate on another occasion, when we were shooting a wood on my Yorkshire property. It was due to the recklessness of a noble lord. We had shot most of the covert, except the last 400 yards or thereabouts; and notwithstanding that I had placed three or four stops at the end, the pheasants still kept flying away 200 yards out of shot. In consequence I suggested to Lord Macdonald, who was walking on the upper side of the hanging covert while I was at the bottom, not above 40 yards from him, that he had better go on to where the stops were as he would then act as another stop, and kill a good many of the birds which were getting away out of shot. He could distinctly see me and all the beaters; moreover my keeper, a very tall man, was walking behind me.

Just as Lord Macdonald started a jay flew up, and to our surprise he turned round and shot at it, although it was in line with the beaters and myself. He shot through the top of the keeper's hat, fortunately without hurting the man, and one pellet hit me just in the beginning of the ball of my eye. I did not make any observation because our shooting would so soon be over, and if I had spoken it would have put an end at once to the day's sport. I was nearly blind of it only half an hour afterwards, and when I got home was obliged to send for a surgeon. He had great doubts whether I should not lose the eye; and as it was a long time passed before I recovered the full sight of it. The pellet at this moment is still in me, but the mishap having occurred so many years ago it has worked its way out of the flesh into the skin and is plainly visible.

I must do Lord Mcdonald the justice to say that nobody could have been more vexed with himself, nor have expressed more sincere regret. He was a very gentlemanly and fine man, full of fun and larking.

Mention of my use of a donkey to shoot off reminds me of a match Lord Middleton made. He had some discussion with a gentleman who was staying with him about the skill of his gamekeeper, and it was agreed that his lordship and the keeper should shoot a match, one of the conditions being that each should carry what the other shot. The man was a very good shot, and after a time Lord Middleton, very tired with the load he had to carry, felt that he must be beaten, as the keeper had not such a weight on his back. So he remembered the terms of the match, and deliberately shot a young donkey, which he insisted the keeper must carry. I was not present and do not know how they settled it, but I suppose the decision would depend on the wording of the articles. If each shooter was to carry 'everything' his opponent killed, Lord Middleton might claim the match.

Lord Middleton was very eccentric; people used to say he was half-mad, but it is not difficult to earn that reputation; it can be done by doing things nobody else does; and Lord Middleton did things which surprised his neighbours. I will mention one; he was a great breeder of cattle, and among his stock had a beautiful prize bull of which he was very proud. It was very docile for a bull, and his lordship took it into his head to shoot partridges off its back. I was told the bull behaved perfectly, taking no notice whatever of the report of its rider's gun....

On the subject of dogs Osbaldeston wrote:

While writing of dogs I recalled a little incident which shows how absurdly some men behave about them. It was at a shooting party at Lord Scarborough's place and among the guests was a tall, fashionable dandy by the name of Teesdale or Tisdale, I forget which, who brought with him a favourite retriever he called Zillah. His solicitude for Zillah made him a laughing stock; he was anxious about Zillah's dinner. Zillah slept in his bedroom. Zillah must not be allowed to get tired. Going out one morning we went in a small omnibus, quite a new vehicle and very well upholstered; the ground was muddy and Teesdale was concerned for Zillah and was chaffed about having a retriever whose feet must not get wet. He was quite serious about it and insisted that his dog must come inside the omnibus, which the shooters completely filled. To this we all objected, pointing out that the vehicle was new and very expensively fitted up, apart from the fact that there really was no room. Teesdale was very indignant, but when somebody gravely suggested that the earl should send into Ollerton, three miles away, for a chaise in which to convey Zillah comfortably, he yielded so far as to let the dog go on the box between the coachman's legs.

I don't know who Teesdale could have been in the habit of shooting with, for when we took our places he kept crying out; 'Take care you don't shoot Zillah!' as if we were all perfect duffers. He went on in this way, and further annoyed his neighhbours by shooting across them, so one of the party took a rise out of him. Zillah's master was not a good shot and she was not at all highly broken; and as he did not give her much to do she wandered away to see what others had killed, thus was often out of Teesdale's sight. The man I mentioned took an opportunity to imitate exactly the cries of pain a dog might utter if wounded; he did it very cleverly and then began to shout 'By Jove! you have shot Zillah,' and went on abusing the imaginary offender for his carelessness. Teesdale rushed up in a most furious passion, demanding; 'What scoundrel has shot my dog! Show me the man who shot my dog!' Fortunately Zillah appeared, from quite a different direction, before any mischief was done. A man in a great rage with a loaded gun is not safe.

Teesdale satisfied himself that his dog had not a mark on her, but he was almost as angry at the trick played on him as he was when he believed she had been shot.

I did not at any time feel inclined to ask Teesdale to shoot and he told us a story of his doings which made me less disposed to do so than before. He was invited to shoot by a friend whose coverts contained much game, and the gentleman, before the party began operations, requested that no hens should be shot. Teesdale did not explain why he did what he told us he did do; he said only the prohibition made him determined to kill everything he could. After shooting for some time he saw pheasants flying away out of shot, and feeling certain that no stops had been placed on purpose that the hens might escape, he went to the spot and found a dry ditch along which the birds were running in numbers. He then made Zillah lie down in the ditch to act as a stop, and when the pheasants rose all round him for a considerable time he killed a great number, most of which were hens. He did not tell us what his host said to him, nor whether he had been invited to shoot there again.

Osbaldeston was revealing about the amount of game killed when muzzle loaders were still the only guns available and when most of the shooting was over dogs.

I had good shooting at Ebberston. The partridge ground within three miles of the house was not equal to some other parts of Yorkshire, nor at all equal to Norfolk and Dorsetshire, but it was very good. I commenced shooting there one year, about the 21st or 22nd of September, hunting setters and pointers. Beginning at seven o'clock in the morning I shot till six, employing neither men nor boys to drive the birds, and did not walk them up with a retriever, as the present custom is in the crack countries. I had two guns and my keeper loaded them, and my dog-breaker hunted the dogs, which were probably better broken than almost any person's. On the day I mention I killed 95 brace of partridges, 28 hares and eight or nine rabbits. I believe if the ground had been driven and dogs not used I might have killed 140 brace.

It had been a good breeding season; I had shot the same ground for many seasons in the same manner, and never before killed above 60 brace. Of course the land was well preserved. I employed five keepers and also watchers, and we had a great deal of game.

We had large numbers of pheasant in the plantations near the house, and within a mile of it. Friends used to visit me from the south as well as from our own county; on one occasion I had staying with me, Lord Huntingfield, who had the reputation of being the best shot in England, The Revd. Mr Hanbury, of Swaffham in Norfolk, and Mr Montague, my nephew, both of whom were first rate shots. The snow was very deep — above our knees on the level — and in consequence of a further fall which did not terminate until noon, we did not commence shooting until nearly one o'clock. We shot in the plantations near the house, and others within half a mile of them, finishing a little after four, the days being very short. On that afternoon we killed 300 pheasants and 100 hares, besides rabbits, of which we kept no count....

Those Regency sportsmen did not spare themselves, or their animals. Lord Kennedy, a notorious gambling man and sportsman, a contemporary of Osbaldeston with whom he was often involved in wagers once;

backed himself for 1, 000 guineas to shoot forty brace of grouse and ride from his shooting quarters at Feloar, in Perthshire, to his house, Dunnottur, near Stonehaven, Aberdeenshire, and back to Feloar in a day. He started very early, rain falling all the time. He killed forty brace by 9 a.m., changed his dress on the hill-side, and mounted a very clever hack, on which he rode the first seven or eight miles. There was no road for that distance; but thence there was a tolerable road to Dunnottur along which he had relays of horses. From Feloar to Dunnottur is about 80 miles. He got back to Feloar at 8 p.m. having shot 40 brace of grouse and ridden 160 miles in less than 15 hours and was not in the least knocked up by it.

One must assume that he was certainly using percussion caps, not flints, but, even so, with muzzle loaders, despite almost certainly having a loader or possibly two standing by, this was a remarkable performance by any standards. It is likely that the shooting was early in August when there were plenty of young birds available and that he was not particular about sparing cheepers, even so the sheer physical effort involved must have been considerable. Although the sums wagered on such occasions were often extremely large the sporting abilities of the participants involved was still exceptional by any standards.

It is surprising how different various accounts of the same shooting day, or sporting events may be seen through different eyes and the following accounts of the same sporting wager from two differing angles, although technically both on

31

the same side, are a very good case in point. 'The Squire of All England', as he was widely and popularly known, or George Osbaldeston of Ebberston in Yorkshire, was a well-known all-round sportsman, and his friend Captain Horatio Ross, a somewhat anglicized Scot, was undoubtedly one of the finest shots of the day. The former was a fairly typical Yorkshireman in most respects, prepared to bristle up in his own defence at any imagined slight, but a genuine sportsman and all-rounder in every sense of the word, who knew and understood dogs and horses as well as shooting, hunting and numerous other sports. Captain Horatio Ross was a brilliant shot, but like many such acknowledged experts was jealous of his own reputation and outside shooting was not so much of a sportsman. The two accounts are barely recognizable as being of the same events.

The Holkham Wager
Captain Horatio Ross's Account

In the year 1824 or 1825 Lord Kennedy and Mr William Coke (nephew of the then Mr Coke of Holkham) shot a match at partridges for a considerable bet. The terms were that Lord Kennedy was to shoot for two days in Scotland against Mr William Coke, who was to shoot for two days at Holkham. Mr Coke, of course, won the match.

I paid a visit to Holkham a month or two after this, and I found them all rather pleased at the result. I could not refrain from saying that Mr Coke must attribute his success more to the number of birds at Holkham than to his being a better shot than Lord Kennedy, for if they met on equal terms I felt perfectly certain he would not stand a ghost of a chance with his lordship. This led ultimately to a match being made between Mr Coke and myself to come off at Holkham the following year. Terms; Mr Coke sen., to name the two 'beats'; a day to intervene between the first and the second day's shooting, to allow the partridges to settle, when we were to change beats; to start as early as we pleased; to load our guns; to hunt the dogs and pick all the birds killed; to be allowed two attendants to help us in any way except picking up the birds, hunting the dogs or loading, as before named.

On my way to Holkham, the following year, I paid a visit to 'the Squire' at Ebberston. I had lost by madness most of my good dogs, and those I had brought with me were indifferent, ill-broken animals. With his usual kindness 'the Squire' said he would lend me his dogs, and I went out with them for a day or two to get acquainted with them. I can say that in Yorkshire they were perfection, but it proved quite another case in Norfolk. The dogs were sent off to Holkham, and 'the Squire' and I followed, he having agreed to act as my umpire. The day after our arrival the two beats selected by Mr Coke were pointed out to us. I tossed with Mr William Coke for the choice and he won the toss.

Next morning we were up before daylight. I was accompanied by Captain Greville R.N. as Mr Coke's umpire. Never shall I forget my start. I entered a turnip-field and away went 'the Squire's' fleet, high-bred dogs, and, almost before they had got half-way down the field, away went (I really believe) four or five hundred partridges at the end of it. The dogs found a scent under every turnip; they were totally bewildered and in a few minutes 'lost their noses' altogether. They rushed here and they rushed there — partridges were rising every moment; they 'backed', they jumped in the air in their excitement, trying to catch the birds, and finally rushed after some, giving tongue like hounds. They followed them into the next turnip field and cleared it also. It was very trying and provoking, but at the same time was so absurd that Captain Greville and I burst out laughing. However, time was passing and I had not as yet fired a shot and I heard my opponent hard at work. I sent my two attendants to try to catch the dogs and in about half an hour they returned with them in couple. I then put a man each side, and walked through the fields, and at sunset had bagged forty brace.

On my way to the Hall a fine old farmer joined me — a Mr Denny. He said he was one of Mr Coke's principal tenants, but in spite of that he could not bear to see me defeated by mere bad luck and ignorance of the country; that I was the best shot they had ever seen, but that I knew no more how to work Norfolk partridges than a child and that I must be beaten unless I altered my system. He then told me that his farm was the one on which I was to shoot the second day and that if I would call on him the next forenoon (i.e in the intervening day) he would give me some hints that would be useful. On reaching the Hall I found that Mr Coke had killed fifty-four brace so that I started the second day fourteen brace behind him.

Next day I called on Mr Denny and we rode over the farm and his instructions were; 'Early in the morning ride the stubble all round this field (a very large field of turnips which he pointed out) and drive the birds into it. I will lend you two old setters which have only two eyes between them; and they will potter about within fifteen and twenty yards, and will help you to find the dead birds. Place your men one each side and beat the field in small circles. If you go straight through it the birds will run to the end and then rise in one great pack; but by making small circles you will cut them off and get shots. The large field will keep you going until 9 o'clock and then go to another large field of turnips' (which he showed me).

I followed the old gentleman's instructions to the letter. I got fifty shots in the first field and by 9 o'clock had bagged fifty partridges. I missed one shot but killed two at one shot afterwards. The result of the day's shooting was that I bagged 59 brace. Mr Coke 36; so that on the two day's shooting I was 9 brace ahead.

Mr W. Coke was not a first class shot, but he was a perfect sportsman. He thoroughly understood how to get at game and although he was not so accurate in his shooting as some of the acknowledged great shots of the day, he was very quick and, as a general rule, killed more game when he went out than other people did. He also had dogs that were perfectly adapted for Norfolk shooting. They were bred between setters and water spaniels. When on a scent they never pointed but went on, their tails straight out, and put their birds up; but as they were broken to keep within twenty-five to thirty yards of Mr Coke they did no harm by flushing in their free and easy manner. They dropped to shot and retrieved dead and wounded birds beautifully and I thought at the time if I had them instead of 'the Squire's' high-bred pointers I would have made a better bag the first day.

Osbaldeston's Account

The match took place at Holkham (18th and 20th October 1825). I was Ross's umpire and the terms were these; Each man to hunt his own dogs and pick up his own game. At that period I had some of the best pointers and setters in the world; for a dog and a bitch, Mark and Flirt (brother and sister), I was offered and refused 100 guineas. I had also three setters of one litter, all excellent; the dog, which I called Jack, was a wonder in his way. I have sometimes had four or five birds down at a time and when this happened he would sit on his rump and mark the spot where each fell; and immediately he heard the ramrod returned he would make for the several birds and retrieve every one even if only winged, through fresh coveys of which he would take no notice. To the best of my belief he never lost a bird in his life. The setters were black and white, the pointers the same.

The Captain and I took a moor together in Scotland the same season and a friend of his lent him some dogs which had the reputation of being the best in England. Ross had never seen mine then. My dog breaker was named Wood; he came out of Kent and brought his setters with him and I purchased them from him. As Ross and I did not shoot together in the Highlands he did not know how good mine were but while there we often talked about the merits of each lot, and at last it ended in my betting him £10 that my dogs got more points than his and were more highly broken. He jumped at the offer; and the result of the trial was that mine beat his hollow, getting nearly two points to one; also my dogs proved themselves as highly broken as was possible, which his were not. I must here name that Wood broke them to the whistle; he could take out two or three brace and when ranging in different lines all would, though they could not see him, drop immediately as if shot. The whistle makes much less noise than the voice and if a dog is not inclined to drop to wing it is very useful.

On our return from Scotland to Ebberston Lodge the Captain commenced partridge shooting and we continued our sport until the end of September when he began to prepare for his match in Norfolk, which was to come off in the middle of October. After the signal defeat of his, or rather his friend's dogs by mine in Scotland, Ross was infatuated with them; he said if he might only be allowed to use them the match was a certainty for him. I told him that perhaps William Coke would not object to such an arrangement but I thought his uncle should be consulted. The Captain therefore wrote to William Coke and the required permission was granted. In those days there was no railroad in existence for Hull and Wood was obliged to bring the dogs on foot; that is to say he rode on a pony and they walked. Their route was by road to Hull and from thence by steamer to Grimsby in Lincolnshire; the journey occupying eight or nine days. We often discussed at my house the merits of my dogs and the hunting of them by whistle and I had particularly impressed upon the Captain the necessity of his becoming well acquainted with them and the different notes used by Wood; it will be remembered that the conditions of the match required each man to hunt his own dogs. Ross was rather indignant at my recommendation, asking if I thought he was a fool who could not manage them as well as Wood. I told him he could not unless he estranged the dogs from the man and practised daily the various notes of the whistle. He would not follow my advice and I believe the issue of the match would have been different had he done so.

When Wood arrived at Hull he had to pass through several back streets and in one of these a seller of earthenware kicked Jack, the setter I valued so highly, in the side. Though the kick was very hard Wood had no reason to suppose the dog had sustained serious injury; but the event proved that Jack was fatally hurt, for he died in the course of the night. I could not avoid dropping a tear in his memory when I heard of it. I felt as if I had lost a child.

Old Mr Coke had not been married very long when Ross and I paid our visit to Holkham. He was I believe, about sixty-nine, and his wife was about twenty-five as near as I could guess. We arrived in sufficient time to dress for dinner, and when we entered the drawing room William Coke introduced us to his uncle. A very large party was assembled and among the elite was His Royal Highness the Duke of Sussex. Mr Coke did not take the least notice of me and his neglect must have been observed by many of the visitors. This, of course, was exceedingly annoying to me. When we sat down to dinner his Royal Highness took his seat near Mrs Coke at the head of the table and old Coke sat at the bottom. As I knew none of the guests I sat by Ross and we might have been four or five places from our host. After dinner Mr Coke asked the Captain many questions, among them: 'Have you had any good shooting this year?' to which Ross replied. 'Yes, at my friend Mr Osbaldeston's.' Mr Coke who had never addressed me at all during dinner, did not even do so then. We adjourned to the drawing room and up to the time of going to bed not a word had passed between the host and myself. They played at whist.

The match extended over two days with an intervening day for rest, and as I was Ross's umpire, William Coke and I breakfasted together in the housekeeper's room as soon as it was light. During our repast I mentioned to Coke how rude his uncle's conduct had been, as if I were an uninvited guest, a regular impudent interloper. He said, 'My uncle is a strange old fellow and he is very annoyed at your dogs being used against me.' I was very much surprised and reminded him that Ross had written for permission to use the dogs and his uncle had granted it immediately, adding that I had a great mind to leave the house and return home.

I felt strongly inclined to take this step, but after consideration, remembering that if I did leave I must take the dogs with me, thus leaving Ross without any, I resolved not to quit the place. The match could not be brought off had I done so, as the articles expressly stipulated that the dogs were to be hunted by the contending parties.

As soon as we had all breakfasted we adjourned to the field of action. Two beats were agreed upon, the arrangement being that each man was to shoot on the other's beat on the second day. Coke used three setters and Ross two setters and three pointers. I may have mentioned that two of the latter were Mark and Flirt, the brother and sister for which I had refused 100 guineas.

Coke, although as I named before, not a first rate shot, killed twelve brace more than the Captain, in consequence of my dogs looking about for their keeper, Wood, instead of minding their business, or obeying Ross, who, moreover, sometimes blew the wrong notes. I had warned him that this would happen if he did not practise with the dogs and learn to hunt them with the whistle's signals to which they were accustomed.

On our return to the house I went immediately up to Ross's room. I found him in the most excited state; he began by blowing me up, saying that I did not make Coke pick up the game and did not see that he killed every bird. I told him that I marked down every bird and produced my list. Then I reproached him for his ingratitude telling him I had had my dogs brought from home, a journey, hither and back of 200 miles, that in thus seeking to help him I had sustained the loss of the most wonderful dog in England and had been insulted by the master of the house. I then left him and retired to my own room to dress. Ross was so exasperated that he did not leave his room for dinner. During the meal old Coke never spoke a word to me.

Soon after we finished, while we were still at the table, the Captain appeared; he sat down nearly opposite me and within three or four places of our host who presently addressed him in these terms; 'Captain Ross, you ought not to feel annoyed at the issue of today's shooting; you shot magnificently, but your dogs — looking at me — are infamous.'

I considered this a good opportunity to give him a rap over the knuckles for the unhandsome manner in which he had behaved to me and observed. 'I beg leave to remind you, Mr Coke, that the dogs are mine, and you know it, as your permission was asked, through your nephew and granted immediately. Now, Sir, infamous as they are, I will bet any person present £500 that I kill tomorrow 50 brace hunting them on the same ground on which the Captain today killed only 40. Or I will shoot any man in Norfolk with them for £1,000.'

Ross at once said; 'You can't do it!' I rejoined that I would and for £500.

William Coke interposed, saying the sum was too large; and I at once offered to do it for £10 adding that I merely sought to prove whether I was justified in my opinion of the dogs. But even this small bet was not accepted.

The Duke of Sussex, who sat next to Mrs Coke at the head of the table seemed uncommonly interested in the discussion and directly asked me to drink wine with him. His Royal Highness's kind interference completely silenced the lot and nothing more was said by anyone in reference to my challenges.

The next day, as I have said, was a rest day. On the third operations were again commenced. William Coke, as before mentioned, was twelve brace ahead and old Mr Coke considered the match as good as won by his nephew in consequence. The Duke of Sussex accompanied by gentlemen and several ladies in carriages came to see the triumph of William Coke. He shot badly on this day and completely lost his temper with his dogs on several occasions. He took them up in his hands and then dashed them down on the ground, swearing the while in the most extraordinary manner; and then in an instant would begin to laugh. I could not help laughing too.

As soon as the party arrived — two or three hours after the shooting had commenced — old Coke came up to me and said: 'Sir, how is my nephew getting on?' to which I replied, 'Anyone who misses more shots than he kills, can't expect to beat Captain Ross.' The Captain, thinking he had discovered a new system (but it was quite an old one) had got the farmers to drive the partridges and he walked them up, using one of my pointers as a retriever, forgetting that this was diametrically opposed to the terms of the articles of the match, viz; 'Each man is to hunt his own dogs and pick up his own game.'

The two were shooting not above half a mile apart and when I was informed of Ross's proceedings I sent a messenger to remind him he was infringing the terms of the match and Mr William Coke could claim it even if Ross killed more birds. He, however, took no notice of my communication and continued to shoot in the same manner. In the evening at the close he was leading by fourteen brace on the day which made him the winner by two brace.

After dinner was finished the circumstances were regularly gone into by the respective parties and they finally agreed to consider the match a draw. To give the devil his due, as they say, old Mr Coke in the handsomest manner, said to the Captain,' Although you have virtually lost the match by not hunting your dogs but merely treading the birds up, and using one dog as a retriever, yet, as you have killed more partridges than my nephew, I will consent to the match being null and void.'

Colonel Peter Hawker was a heavy dragoon and his methods of shooting game were based on his experiences as a soldier in the Peninsular Campaign. Even in those days they were unusual. He employed a dozen or more followers, some mounted, some on foot, who spread out on either side of Hawker himself and were also posted at various vantage points round about. Hawker, usually alone, but sometimes with a reliable companion, would be mounted on horseback with two pointers quartering the ground. When the dogs came on point Hawker would dismount, the covey would be flushed and one or more birds shot. The flight of the birds would be observed by his followers and Hawker would then ride at full speed to the place where they had pitched. The covey would be pointed again and another bird, or birds shot. This would continue until the exhausted birds could barely fly and Hawker was particularly pleased if he could shoot two, or more birds at a time when crossing in flight, terming this a cannon. Shooting the birds as soon as they had cleared the stubbles was considered essential and shots of up to seventy yards were often taken with heavily choked muzzle loaders. Hawker was also not above shooting out of a carriage window with a duck gun at times. Securing the game in the bag was the important aim regardless of the methods employed. Starting around nine in the morning he was quite prepared to shoot on up to eight, even at times until darkness was falling, simply to achieve a round number of birds. Modern concepts of sportsmanship, or any sense of feeling for the game he hunted, appeared to be totally lacking. He would cheerfully count birds shot but unpicked as 'in the bag' to make his final figures more impressive. The following records are taken direct from the original diaries now, sadly, only to be had by recourse to the librarian of the Yale Library. Both Sir Ralph Payne Gallwey and Eric Parker, who edited his diaries have glossed over some of the original entries. Here is his account of shooting near his home at Longparish and later near his house on the Hampshire coast at Keyhaven in 1827.

Longparish 1827

September 1st — The greatest day on record here. 102 partridges and 1 hare besides 3 brace more birds shot and lost.

N.B: A cold, dry, strong easterly wind, with no scent, but I took care to have a fine army of cavalry and infantry and made ample allowance for the wildness of the birds by the rapidity of our charges. I had no dogs but poor old Duchess and Sappho, both like myself among the 'has beens.' I started at noon but had the first 'butcher's halloo' or three cheers for 20 brace at two. A second 'butcher's halloo' at twenty minutes before six, and I then worked like a slave for the glory of making up 50 brace off my own gun, which I not only did, but on turning out the game, it proved I had miscounted and had gone one brace over the desired number. I believe under all circumstances and at all events in our district, this nearly doubles any day on record in the annals of its sporting history.

2nd Sunday. Nothing so fortunate as this because it keeps all the raw fools off and allows the birds a little time to forget what has passed.

3rd. 50 partridges and 2 hares; the greatest second day in my annals. A still stronger easterly wind. The ground like rocks of stone and the dust flying like Irish snuff. Birds walking about like poultry; and so wild that even in the rushes and woods they would not stay to be fired at, but kept running off like hares; and in short, nothing could be done with them until they were dispersed by cavalry and infantry, the labour of which made the day more like a hot and severe action than a day's sport and pleasure. Every man, dog and horse was so exhausted as to be quite knocked up.

4th. Busy ticketing off a houseful of game...heard that no-one around had done a fourth what I had. My whole army much exhausted and a general resting day. A few shooters popping about, but nothing done. There rarely ever is after a grand field day, as the birds have not recovered their nerves to settle quietly.

5th. Another general resting day; men, horses, dogs and birds still unfit for war...

6th. At them again. Another brilliant and unprecedented day. 56 partridges and 3 hares.

N.B. — A cold, dry, easterly wind, with a scorching sun again; never found a bird for the first hour, but at last discovered that the main army of the partridges had retrenched themselves in a piece of thick clover on the estate of Sir Henry Wilson, of not more than three acres. His friend and steward, Captain Clark, kindly gave me leave to enter this garrison of game, and directed me to give them no quarter; so in this one little field I bagged 10 brace of birds and 1 hare without missing a shot. Indeed this was the only sport; like easy September shooting I have seen this season. The birds then returned to and dispersed on my own shooting ground which was well planted with markers and here we did gloriously. But had it not been for this lucky circumstance I doubt whether we should have made a good day's sport; and I am quite sure we should have been puzzled to make up 200 head of game in three days which everyone was anxious I should do. As it was, however, I made up 214 head of game in three days' shooting viz; 1st 102 partridges and 1 hare; 3rd 50 partridges and 2 hares; 6th 56 partridges and 3 hares; Total 208 partridges and 6 hares. Making 214 head besides lost birds.

I every day returned home with my cavalry and infantry in proper form of procession, instead of allowing them to straggle in like a vanquished army or disorderly banditti, which attracted no small admiration and laughter amongst the friends who were with me.

Having now done what I believe never was done here before, and what may possibly never be done here again, and supplied all the farmers and my friends with game, I shall here terminate the war against the partridges; and, at all events, leave them to others till I want game again and can have proper scenting weather to kill a few birds in a quiet way.

15th. Mr Childe the artist arrived at Longparish and Mr Joseph Manton preparative of a painting being made of our *partie de chasse.*

17th. Assembled my myrmidons for one more grand field day. In order to have some of their likenesses, Mr Childe attended as a strict observer and Mr Joseph Manton shot with me. Our united bag was 48 partridges and 1 hare, and we returned some time before the day was over in order that Mr Childe might complete by good daylight the necessary sketches of the group. My share of the bag was 29 partridges but had I shot entirely by myself and been able to waive the usual ceremony of shooting in company, and galloped up to all my birds as heretofore, I am confident I should have killed 30 brace of birds. I therefore calculate that by taking out another sportsman the larder fell 6 brace short; because to follow up birds as I ought in this wild country, I must do that which in any company would be unsportsmanlike and ungentlemanlike to whoever was my companion; and Joe Manton, not being one of the quickest movers, either on horseback or on foot doubly retarded several of the necessary attacks.

25th. Tremendous gale of wind all day, with occasional showers. Everyone laughed at me for going out. However I worked 10 brace of birds...and all within less than four hours; having bagged (besides 4 towered and lost birds) 20 partridges and 1 snipe. And all done by dint of rapid snap shooting.

27th. I pottered out on a pony to get a few more birds in a quiet; but I was forced to quack myself up for the sortie with Huxham's bark and sal volatile. I started at half-past twelve and came in at half past four with 24 partridges, 3 snipes and the only landrail I have seen or heard of this year (besides 4 more birds shot and lost) and *all without once missing a shot!* though in spite of beautiful weather the birds were so wild that half those I fired at were snap shots. I made five double shots and three cannons in the course of the day; and under all circumstances consider this the best day's sport I have had this season; N.B. Including the 4 lost birds I killed this makes 32 head of game in 29 shots: because the making of 3 cannons (two at a shot crossing) gave me 3 times two birds to one barrel!

...Game killed in September 1827.

(N.B My two old worn out bitches were the only dogs I had to shoot with!)...Partridges 330; Hares 10; Snipes 4; Landrail 1. Total 345 head. (Besides about 12 brace shot dead and lost to say nothing of wounded birds.) This is the best sport I ever had...tho' far from being in good health I never shot better...

October

...10th. Proceeded to Southampton for the day to inspect and direct the progress of a *ne plus ultra* new punt, and at night went on and arrived at (my healthiest of homes) Keyhaven. *It poured with rain the whole day;* but as I was either in chaises, or inside the coach, I escaped getting wet...

17th. Got my maiden shot of the season, from which I picked up 2 brent geese, 2 pintails, and 1 wigeon; and these were all the birds I had to fire at, except 1 other goose, that went off severely hit and dropped off at sea. (These 3 are the first geese that have been heard of this season and very early it is for them! — I therefore sent the produce of this maiden shot, with what little game I had, to the Lord High Admiral.)

I then came home and went game shooting. — All I saw was a covey of 6 partridges, out of which I killed a very brilliant double shot, but I lost my second barrel bird. At the close of the day, however, I made up my 2 partridges bagged, by kicking up an old strong cock and *flooring* him in Mr Davison's potatoes. Then we had *quite an event* with an old hare, an animal that is thought as much of at Keyhaven as an elephant. I let fly at her a scrambling shot, a long way off, and through the potatoes; down she came, and the dog had hold of her. Off she set again; and so red with blood that she actually appeared as if hooded in scarlet. Bagshot, Mr Davison, myself and a whole banditti had a chase after her for nearly half an hour, till, at last, we gave her up. Soon after she was *chased by an old woman* who caught her by the breeches and let her go in a fright when she began to squeal, for fear that she (the said old woman) should be scratched. Then we heard that this wonderful hare had run into someone's house and Lord knows how many stories. In short she was cut all to pieces and is, no doubt, dead; and she was the first living creature that I had pulled the trigger at, without bagging, since my arrival at this place. After this *rum* affair I went home, shipped water boots, shifted my shot and went out for snipes. All I fired at was a snipe and a jack snipe, (both of which I bagged, long shots) except discharging my gun at and killing, a *swallow;* just to say that I had *shot wild geese and a swallow on the same day!!!* Here ended my *3 heterogeneous sallies* in shooting this *day;* and at night my waggon, with my workman, *Admiral* Buckle, and all the traps for finishing the new light punt arrived...

24th. About 20 wigeon dropped in off Pennington Lake. Reade and I went off to them in the 'Lion'. I let fly both barrels and *stopped 12 of them* at about 110 yards, but it was so rough that I lost nearly all my cripples; and in short came in with but 5 wigeon, with which I had every reason to be satisfied.

25th. A gale of wind and rain all the morning. In the evening it abated and we tried the new punt in an unfinished state (just to 'trim her on all tacks') and nothing could answer more beautifully than she did! While busy at the punt a very fine fat knot pitched on the salt-pans and I ran in for my musket and got him. This was the only shot I fired today except a capital one at a mark from the new punt...'

As already noted Colonel Peter Hawker's book on shooting published in 1816 *Instructions to Young Sportsman in all that relates to Guns and Shooting* ran into numerous editions. The following is from the sixth edition of his book, dated 1830.

I shall leave the following directions as they originally stood, for flint-guns; repeating my observation that, with *detonaters,* the young sportsman has only to make *half* the allowance at crossing objects, &c.

Let every one, who begins shooting, take warning from the many serious misfortunes, that have, alas! too often occurred, and start with the *determination* of *never suffering a gun, at any time, to be held for a moment,* or even *carried,* so as to be *likely to come in the direction of either man or beast.* One who strictly abides by this *golden rule,* would be less liable to accidents, even if he *went from his door* with *both barrels cocked,* than he, who neglected it...

He later compared different forms of shooting as follows:

...one man goes out and springs birds enough to fire fifty times, within forty yards, and perhaps, being a *reputation* shooter, only twenty of these shots happen to suit his fancy. He never fires a second barrel unless the birds rise one at a time, or a covey happens to spring from under his feet; and, in short, he kills his twenty birds in twenty shots. The other man takes the whole of the fifty shots, many of which may be very difficult ones, and under extreme disadvantages; he kills thirty-five, and misses fifteen. A fair sportsman and really good judge, I conceive, would not hesitate to say, that the latter has claim to be considered the better shot of the two.

We will then bring a first-rate shot into the field, and he shall kill forty-five out of the fifty (never failing, of course, to work both his barrels on every fair occasion): he will then have missed five times; and would any old sportsman judge so unfairly as to place *before him* the *never-miss gentleman* with his twenty trap shots running?...

With regard to the *distance,* which constitutes *a fair shot,* there is no speaking precisely; but as far as such things can be *brought to paper,* and *guns to an average,* I should say that, provided a gun is held straight, a bird should scarcely ever escape at *forty yards*; and that is the *outside* of *point-blank* range, although, at *fifty yards,* the chances are *three to one in favour of killing,* with a *good aim*; but as a gun *never shoots twice alike,* a bird, at *this* distance may *sometimes* be struck with *three or four shot,* and at *others* may *escape through an interval,* though the piece be never so well directed. But, if a pellet should take a bird in a *vital part,* or *the wing,* at *seventy* or even *eighty yards,* it would probably come down, though the odds at such distances are, of course, against your hitting it at all. Birds *flying straight away,* or *coming to you,* require a *much harder blow,* than those *crossing,* or *flying directly over your head;* by reason that, in the *first* instance, they are partly *shielded by the rump* and, in the *second,* the *feathers* are apt, at long distances, to *glance the shot....*

When two persons are shooting together, there cannot be a more simple way of avoiding confusion than for each man, when a covey rises, to select the outer birds on his own side. Let all birds that cross belong exclusively to that shooter for whose side their heads are pointed; and let all single birds, that may rise and go away fair for either person, be *taken alternately*, and *left entirely for the two barrels of the shooter to whom they belong.* By this means there is no *'wiping of noses!'* as they call it; no *'blazing a volley into the brown of 'em!'* or in other words, no jealousy; no unfair work; and two sportsmen may thus shoot coolly together with good nerves and in good friendship, instead of with jealousy and greediness, which not only destroys all pleasure, but soon lessens their good shooting, if not their good fellowship. I adopted these regulations for three seasons, with one of the best shots that ever went into a field; and our diversion, by this means, invariably went so pleasantly, that we shot with additional confidence when in each other's company...

As a further proof of the quickness with which two barrels may be correctly fired, *provided the gun is kept to the shoulder,* I shall mention an instance — Mr Ford, gamekeeper to the Earl of Portsmouth, and a man about *six feet six! laid his gun on the ground,* of course with both barrels cocked; and, after *throwing* off two penny pieces *himself,* he *took up his gun,* and hit them both most handsomely, before either fell to the ground. He requested me to try, with his gun, if I could do the same. At first I failed, for want of being, what we used to call at Eton, a good *'shy;'* but, after Ford had given me a few lessons in the throwing department, I did it the first time (though, perhaps, more by luck than skill), putting five shot in one, and six in the other; which led me to conclude that, by *practice,* this might be reduced to about the same degree of certainty as other quick double shots. As to a man with his gun in his hand, throwing up, and hitting, two-penny pieces, or halfpence, it is no more than what many good shots can do, by the mere knack *of catching the first just after the turn and presenting well under the second:* but the other performance is really a difficulty. Let some of the pigeon-shooters try this, by way of a 'spree' and they will save a good deal of innocent blood, and find they have enough to do. Most people will say, 'This is not like shooting *birds.'* — True, but I say this, — it distinguishes, to speak musically, the *prestissimo* from the *allegro,* in *handling a double gun...*

In his *Instructions to Young Sportsmen,* Hawker gave somewhat dubious, but also interesting, instructions on choosing and preserving game:

Although it is not meant to dwell here on a subject which more properly belongs to a *cookery* book, yet it would be very hard not to have some consideration for many, who would rather see a bird roasted and well frothed up on a table, than ten thousand springing from a stubble, or feeding under the moon. Let it therefore be observed that, in *choosing* birds, you cannot be guided better than by selecting those, which of their kind, are the *heaviest* in weight and the least beautiful in plumage.

Young birds may be distinguished by the *softness* of their *quills* which in *older* ones, will be *hard* and *white.* The females are, in general, preferable to the males; they are more juicy and seldom so tough. For example a hen pheasant (provided it is not a very *dark-coloured* one, which would denote its being an *old barren hen.* Such birds, by the way, should always be destroyed as *vermin* because they take to *sucking the eggs* of the others) or a duck is to be preferred to a cock pheasant or a mallard. The *old pheasants* may be distinguished by the *length and sharpness* of their spurs, which in the younger ones, are short and blunt. Old partridges are always to be known, during the *early part of the season,* by their legs being of a *pale blue,* instead of a yellowish brown; so that when a Londoner receives his brace of blue-legged birds in September, he should immediately *snap their legs and draw out the sinews*, by means of *pulling off the feet* instead of leaving them to torment him, like so many strings, when he would be wishing to enjoy his repast. This remedy of *making the leg tender* removes the objection to old birds, provided the weather will admit of their being sufficiently kept; and indeed they are often preferable, from having a high flavour. If birds are overkept their *legs* will be *dry, their eyes much sunk,* and the *vent,* will become soft and somewhat *discoloured.* The *first place* to ascertain if they are beginning to be *high* is the *inside of their bills,* where it is not amiss to put some heather straw, or spice, if you want to keep them for any length of time. Birds that have *fallen in the*

45

water or have not had time to get *cold* should never be packed like others, but sent *openly* and dressed as soon as possible. Partridges are often spoiled in September by being put to ferment in a large bag or pannier, which is carried by men on horseback. It may perhaps be asked by some one, on seeing the frontispiece, why are the partridges carried on a pole? The reason is this: — when you put many birds together in a bag, when the weather is hot, and fag about with them, *particularly on horseback* the *under* ones, at all events, are only fit for *entrees* or cats' meat. If you hang them up in anything — still they are liable to be shook, as well as have *their heads pulled off.* But a pole, from requiring two people, cannot be otherwise than steadily carried; and thus your birds are kept cleaner than by other means...

Sportsmen are often heartily abused by their acquaintance (I cannot bring myself to hackney the word *friends* quite so fluently as I ought to do) for sending them 'tough and good-for-nothing game,' while all the blame should, in many instances, rest with themselves, or their pudding-headed cook, who maybe dresses an old pheasant, or hare the very day after it was killed, or perhaps while engrossed in a story or argument, leaves it to roast away till there remains neither juice nor flavour.

All game &c should be kept till properly tender, or, *if wanted in a hurry*, it may be picked, wrapped up in a cloth, and *thus buried* in the earth for a few hours before it is dressed. This is the custom abroad, where I have supped on wildfowl, *perfectly tender*, that were killed since an early dinner on the same day.

Birds that are dressed so soon after being killed, as scarcely to have become cold, are more tender than if put by for a night and afterwards not kept long enough. On the other hand, if you want them kept a very long time, for any particular purpose, powdered charcoal (for game, venison, or anything) is the best recipe I have been able to procure.

Keep your game in a *safe* or well secured larder, to avoid *flies*: and to get rid of *rats* you have only to leave out, for their supper a *red herring*, which you must first split open, and then occasionally heat before the fire, while you put over and into it about as much *corrosive sublimate of mercury* as would lie on a half-crown. The rats, when they have eaten this, will shortly afterwards adjourn to the water; and, instead of returning, there drink themselves to death. This is a far more certain recipe to destroy rats than the mercurial ointment, which was before named in this work. It may be worthwhile to observe also *en passant*, that the corrosive sublimate of mercury is a *never failing remedy to destroy bugs*, if mixed with spirits of wine, and well worked, with a paint brush, into the joints and crevices of furniture. But you can never depend on completely annihilating the *breed* of them, till you do away with the papering of the walls of town bed-rooms.

N.B. *Be very careful how you handle, or where you leave, this preparation, it being* POISON.

Q. What has this last recipe to do with *sporting?*

A. The citizens have been enlightening us country shooters with a new system of instructions for killing *our game*, and therefore the least I can do in return is give them a short recipe for killing *theirs*....

Hares and rabbits *when old* have blunt claws; are broad across the back; their ears are very tough; and when cut their *flesh curls up* and remains dry. The first joint of their foreleg is larger and stiffer than in young ones, and their jawbones are very hard. In *young* hares and rabbits all is the *reverse* to this; *their* ears are easily torn and *their* jawbones may be cracked with the forefinger and thumb.

The game laws were overdue for change and in 1827 a start was made with the prohibition of spring-guns and mantraps. In 1828 the Night Poaching Act was passed, by which an armed gang of three or more could lay themselves open to a sentence of seven years' transportation to Botany Bay. (This was not abolished until 1867.) On the other hand it was not an offence to trespass at night in search of rabbits, unless they were actually taken or killed.

In 1831 the Game Act introduced by William IV, acting partly on Hawker's advice, revised the entire game laws. The old qualification system was abolished, along with other archaic anomalies. By these revised laws game dealers had to have a licence to deal in game and to some extent this lessened the menace of organized poaching. On the other hand the maximum fines for daytime poaching were fixed at five pounds for shooting game on someone else's land without a licence and two pounds for trespassing in search of game. The more severe sentence for armed night gangs of poachers remained as already set.

Although shooting driven grouse took place on some Yorkshire moors as early as 1805, shooting at this stage was generally still practised over pointers. An exception seems to have been common in Norfolk where the method of driving partridges into large fields of roots and then walking them up in circles to prevent them running out of the drills was often followed. In this way good shots with a couple of quiet steady dogs and a pair of guns each could make some quite startling bags. Indeed when eventually driven shooting came into general usage at Holkham (around 1860 after the introduction of the breech-loader) there was little alteration in the size of the bags. Already, in East Anglia at least, it had been appreciated that game is a crop which should be taken annually according to the numbers available as a result of careful preservation.

Although there were many outstanding sportsmen to be seen in the shooting field in the first half of the nineteenth century it must also be remembered that there were quite a few who were positively dangerous. Charles Dickens in *The Pickwick Papers* provides a memorable picture of a shooting party around 1840 or thereabouts.

Mr Pickwick Goes Partridge Shooting In A Wheelbarrow

The birds, who, happily for their own peace of mind and personal comfort, were in blissful ignorance of the preparations, which had been in making to astonish them, on the first of September, hailed it no doubt as one of the pleasantest mornings they had seen that season...it was a fine morning...when an open carriage, in which were three Pickwickians (Mr Pickwick, Mr Winkle and Mr Tupman), Mr Wardle and Mr Trundle, with Sam Weller on the box beside the driver, pulled up by a gate at the roadside, before which stood a tall raw-boned gamekeeper and a half-booted, leather-leggined boy; each bearing a bag of capacious dimensions, and accompanied by a brace of pointers.

'I say,' whispered Mr Winkle to Wardle, as the man let down the steps, 'they don't suppose we're going to kill enough game to fill those bags, do they?'

'Fill them!' exclaimed old Wardle. 'Bless you, yes! You shall fill one and I the other; and when we've done with them, the pockets of our shooting coats will hold as much more.'

Mr Winkle dismounted without saying anything in reply to this observation; but he thought within himself that if the party remained in the open air, until he had filled one of those bags, they stood a considerable chance of catching colds in their heads.

'Hi Juno, lass — hi, old girl; down Daph, down,' said Wardle, caressing the dogs. 'Sir Geoffrey still in Scotland, of course, Martin?'

The tall gamekeeper replied in the affirmative and looked with some surprise from Mr Winkle who was holding his gun as if he wished his coat pocket to save him the trouble of pulling the trigger, to Mr Tupman, who was holding his as if he was afraid of it — as there is no earthly reason to doubt he really was.

'My friends are not much in the way of this sort of thing yet, Martin,' said Wardle noticing the look. 'Live and learn, you know. They'll be good shots one of these days. I beg my friend Winkle's pardon, though; he has had some practice.'

Mr Winkle smiled feebly over his blue neckerchief in acknowledgement of the compliment and got himself so mysteriously entangled with his gun, in his modest confusion, that if the piece had been loaded, he must inevitably have shot himself dead upon the spot.

'You mustn't handle your piece in that ere way, when you come to have the charge in it, sir,' said the tall gamekeeper, gruffly, 'or I'm damned if you won't make cold meat of some on us.'

Mr Winkle, thus admonished, abruptly altered its position, and in so doing contrived to bring the barrel into pretty sharp contact with Mr Weller's head.

'Hallo!' said Sam, picking up his hat, which had been knocked off, and rubbing his temple. 'Hallo, sir! if you come's it this vay, you'll fill one of them bags, and something to spare, at one fire.'

Here the leather-leggined boy laughed very heartily, and then tried to look as if it was somebody else, whereat Mr Winkle frowned majestically.

'Where did you tell the boy to meet us with the snack, Martin?' inquired Wardle.

'Side of One-tree Hill, at twelve o'clock, sir.'...

'Very well,' said old Mr Wardle. 'Now the sooner we're off the better. Will you join us at twelve, then, Pickwick?'

Mr Pickwick was particularly anxious to view the sport, the more especially as he was rather anxious in respect of Mr Winkle's life and limbs. On so inviting a morning, too, it was very tantalising to turn back, and leave his friends to enjoy themselves. It was therefore with a very rueful air that he replied.

'Why, I suppose I must.'

'An't the gentleman a shot, sir?' enquired the long gamekeeper.

'No,' replied Wardle, 'and he's lame besides.'

'I should very much like to go,' said Mr Pickwick, 'very much.'

There was a short pause of commiseration.

'There's a barrow t'other side of the hedge,' said the boy.' If the gentleman's servant would wheel along the paths, he could keep nigh us, and we could lift it over the stiles and that.'

'The wery thing,' said Mr Weller, who was a party interested, inasmuch as he ardently longed to see the sport. 'The wery thing. Well said, Smallcheck; I'll have it out in a minute.'

But here a difficulty arose. The long gamekeeper resolutely protested against the introduction into a shooting party, of a gentleman in a barrow, as a gross violation of all established rules and precedents.

It was a great objection, but not an insurmountable one. The gamekeeper having been coaxed and fee'd, and having, moreover, eased his mind by 'punching' the head of the inventive youth who had first suggested the use of the machine, Mr Pickwick was placed in it, and off the party set; Wardle and the long gamekeeper leading the way, and Mr Pickwick in the barrow, propelled by Sam, bringing up the rear.

'Stop, Sam,' said Mr Pickwick when they had got half across the first field.

'What's the matter now?' said Wardle.

'I won't suffer this barrow to be moved another step,' said Mr Pickwick resolutely, 'unless Winkle carries that gun of his in a different manner.'

'How *am* I to carry it?' said the wretched Winkle.

'Carry it with the muzzle to the ground,' replied Mr Pickwick.

'It's so unsportsman-like,' reasoned Winkle.

'I don't care whether it's unsportsman-like or not,' replied Mr Pickwick; 'I am not going to be shot in a wheelbarrow, for the sake of appearances, to please anybody.'

'I know the gentleman'll put that ere charge into somebody, afore he's done,' growled the long man.

'Well, well — I don't mind,' said poor Winkle, turning his gun-stock uppermost; — 'there.'

'Anything for a quiet life,' said Mr Weller; and on they went again.

'Stop!' said Mr Pickwick, after they had gone a few yards further.

'What now?' said Wardle.

'That gun of Tupman's is not safe; I know it isn't,' said Mr Pickwick.

'Eh? What! not safe?' said Mr Tupman in a tone of great alarm.

'Not as you are carrying it,' said Mr Pickwick. 'I am very sorry to make any further objection, but I cannot consent to go on, unless you carry it as Winkle does his.'

'I think you had better, sir,' said the long gamekeeper, 'or you're quite as likely to lodge the charge in yourself as in anything else.'

Mr Tupman, with the most obliging haste, placed his piece in the position required, and the party moved on again; the two amateurs marching with reversed arms, like a couple of privates at a royal funeral.

The dogs suddenly came to a dead stop, and the party advancing stealthily a single pace, stopped too.

'What's the matter with the dogs' legs?' whispered Mr Winkle. 'How queer they're standing.'

'Hush, can't you?' replied Wardle softly. 'Don't you see, they're making a point?'

'Making a point!' said Mr Winkle, staring about him, as if he expected to discover some particular beauty in the landscape, which the sagacious animals were calling special attention to. 'Making a point! What are they pointing at?'

'Keep your eyes open,' said Wardle, not heeding the question in the excitement of the moment. 'Now then.'

There was a sharp whirring noise, that made Mr Winkle start back as if he had been shot himself. Bang, bang, went a couple of the guns; — the smoke swept quickly away over the field and curled into the air.

'Where are they?' said Mr Winkle, in a state of the highest excitement, turning round and round in all directions. 'Where are they? Tell me when to fire. Where are they — where are they?'

'Where are they?' said Mr Wardle, taking up a brace of birds, which the dogs had deposited at his feet. 'Why, here they are.'

'No, no; I mean the others,' said the bewildered Winkle.

'Far enough off, by this time,' replied Wardle, coolly reloading his gun.

'We shall very likely be up with another covey in five minutes,' said the long gamekeeper. 'If the gentleman begins to fire now, perhaps he'll just get the shot out of the barrel by the time they rise.'

'Ha! ha! ha!' roared Mr Weller.

'Sam,' said Mr Pickwick, compassionating his follower's confusion and embarrassment.

'Sir.'

'Don't laugh.'

'Certainly not, sir.' So, by way of indemnification, Mr Weller contorted his features from behind the wheelbarrow, for the exclusive amusement of the boy with the leggings, who thereupon burst into a boisterous laugh and was summarily cuffed by the long gamekeeper, who wanted a pretext for turning round to hide his own merriment.

'Bravo, old fellow!' said Wardle to Mr Tupman; 'You fired that time at all events.'

'Oh yes,' replied Mr Tupman, with conscious pride. 'I let it off.'

'Well done. You'll hit something next time, if you look sharp. Very easy, ain't it?'

'Yes. It's very easy,' said Mr Tupman. 'How it hurts one's shoulder though. It nearly knocked me backwards. I had no idea these small firearms kicked so.'

'Ah,' said the old gentlemen, smiling; 'You'll get used to it in time. Now then — all ready — all right with the barrow there?'

'All right, sir,' replied Mr Weller.

'Come along then.'

'Hold hard, sir,' said Sam, raising the barrow.

'Aye, aye,' replied Mr Pickwick; and on they went as briskly as need be.

'Keep that barrow back now,' cried Wardle when it had been hoisted over a stile into another field and Mr Pickwick had been deposited in it once more.

'All right, sir,' replied Mr Weller, pausing.

'Now, Winkle,' said the old gentleman, 'Follow me softly, and don't be too late this time.'

'Never fear,' said Mr Winkle. 'Are they pointing?'

'No, no; not now. Quietly, now, quietly.' On they crept, and very quietly they would have advanced, if Mr Winkle, in the performance of some very intricate evolutions with his gun, had not accidentally fired, at the most critical moment, over the boy's head, exactly in the spot where the tall man's brains would have been, had he been there instead.

'Why, what on earth did you do that for?' said old Wardle, as the birds flew unharmed away.

'I never saw such a gun in my life,' replied poor Mr Winkle, looking at the lock, as if that would do any good. 'It goes off of its own accord. It *will* do it.'

'Will do it!' echoed Wardle, with something of irritation in his manner. 'I wish it would kill something of its own accord.'

'It'll do that afore long, sir,' observed the tall man, in a low, prophetic voice.

'What do you mean by that observation, sir?' inquired Mr Winkle, angrily.

'Never mind, sir, never mind,' replied the long gamekeeper. 'I've no family myself, sir; and this here boy's mother will get something handsome from Sir Geoffrey, if he's killed on his land. Load again, sir, load again.'

'Take away his gun,' cried Mr Pickwick, from the barrow, horror-stricken at the long man's dark insinuations. 'Take away his gun, do you hear, somebody?'

Nobody, however, volunteered to obey the command; and Mr Winkle, after darting a rebellious glance at Mr Pickwick, reloaded his gun, and proceeded onwards with the rest.

We are bound, on the authority of Mr Pickwick, to state, that Mr Tupman's mode of proceeding evinced far more of prudence and deliberation, than that adopted by Mr Winkle. Still, this by no means detracts from the great authority of the latter gentleman, on all matters concerned with the field; because, as Mr Pickwick beautifully observes, it has somehow or other happened, from time immemorial, that many of the best and ablest philosophers, who have been perfect lights of science in matters of theory, have been wholly unable to reduce them to practice.

Mr Tupman's process, like many of our most sublime discoveries, was extremely simple. With the quickness and penetration of a man of genius, he had at once observed that the two great points to be attained were — first, to discharge his piece without injury to himself, and, secondly, to do so, without danger to the by-standers; — obviously, the best thing to do, after surmounting the difficulty of firing at all, was to shut his eyes firmly, and fire into the air.

On one occasion, after performing this feat, Mr Tupman, on opening his eyes, beheld a plump partridge in the act of falling wounded to the ground. He was on the point of congratulating Mr Wardle on his invariable success, when that gentleman advanced towards him, and grasped him warmly by the hand.

'Tupman,' said the old gentleman, 'You singled out that particular bird?'

'No', said Mr Tupman — 'no.'

'You did,' said Wardle. 'I saw you do it — I observed you pick him out — I noticed you, as you raised your piece to take aim; and I will say this, that the best shot in existence could not have done it more beautifully. You are an older hand at this, than I thought you, Tupman; you have been out before.'

It was in vain for Mr Tupman to protest, with a smile of self-denial that he never had. The very smile was taken as evidence to the contrary; and from that

time forth, his reputation was established. It is not the only reputation that has been acquired as easily, nor are such fortunate circumstances confined to partridge shooting.

In 1838 William Scrope published *The Art of Deer Stalking,* although the racy picture he presented was rather of deer driving than of stalking. However from this period onwards, with the arrival of Queen Victoria and Prince Albert at Balmoral and following the royal example there was a swing over towards deer stalking as a sport in the Highlands in the 1840s. The following game records are of interest:

'...the unpublished Game Records of Strathconan Estate dated 1841 and ending in the year 1850 still exist, covering...the transitional period when sheep were removed (from the Highlands) to make way for game and deer stalking began to develop in popularity.

Background

The 73, 000 or so acres (29, 554 ha) of Strathconan in Easter Ross, a little south of Strathpeffer were bought as a Highland sporting estate in 1839 by Mr James Balfour of Whittingehame in East Lothian. It is significant that there is no mention of deer in the particulars of sale and the sheep were presumably cleared from it by 1841, the date on the front of the Game Book. Although thus prominently dated 1841, the first year entered is in fact 1842 and the year 1843 is not included presumably because James Maitland Balfour, the heir to the estate, was married that year. The records for the various years are as follows:

1842

Shooting began on 13 August and ended on the 26th during which 505 grouse were shot over dogs. The total head of game noted was 590, including thirty ptarmigan, fourteen black game and four salmon, with no mention of either red or roe deer.

1844

The season ended on the 14 September. On the 10 August Mr James Balfour went out and a note records: 'Shot a stag with 12 points and was going to cut his throat when he got up and ran off.'

On the 12th and 13th 136 grouse were shot over dogs. On the 14th the first red deer was recorded and on the 16th another, but in neither case are details of weight or the number of points on the antlers mentioned. On 28 August an entry reads: 'Mr J. Balfour had a good shot at a stag, but missed.' Another red deer with no further details is recorded shot on the 31st and a fourth on 13 September. Four red deer were thus included in the total of 1647 head of game shot, of which 1510 were grouse.

1845

The season started on 16 August and ended on 20 September. A red deer, with no further details given is noted as shot on the 19th. On 30 August a roebuck is recorded without comment. The entry for 6 September notes: 'Saw 4 stags did not get a shot.' On 8 September: 'Got a shot at 2 stags. Talbot hit one and I think I wounded the other.' The total bag recorded on 20 September was 1723 head of which 1552 were grouse with only one red deer and the roebuck noted.

1846

James Balfour arrived on the 11th and caught a salmon, before opening the grouse season on the 12th. The season ended on 17 September. Sandwiched amongst the records of the grouse shooting are various notes on deer. On 14 August is recorded: 'Saw 6 stags and missed 2 shots.' On 1 September: 'Had a good chance at 5 stags' and without further details one red deer is recorded killed. On 2 September, apparently while shooting grouse, one roe deer is also recorded. On 5 September: 'Missed 2 good stags; wounded another.' On the 10th, without comment, another red deer is listed shot. On the 17th the season ended with just the two red deer and the roe deer recorded in a total of 2765 head shot of which 2395 were grouse.

1847

The shooting party appears to have arrived on 10 August and sport ended on 29 September. On 11 August is the laconic entry: 'Wounded a stag.' On 16 August: 'Saw and missed 10 stags very fine. One a royal.' On the 23rd: 'A very fat stag killed by Sir I. Moncrieffe.' On the 26th another deer is recorded without comment. On 2 September another is shot and the entry reads: 'Wounded three others.' On the 6, 14 and 15 September three further red deer are recorded, but whether they are the three wounded is not recorded. The total is thus six red deer out of 1145 head shot of which 1040 were grouse.

1848

The season opened on 18 August and finished on 11 October. There were only five days shooting in August and six in September so it may be assumed that this was an exceptionally wet year. On 21 September there is the cryptic entry: 'A hind by accident.' Compared with previous years this is by far the worst with only 311 head shot, of which 239 were grouse and the hind represented the sole red deer.

1849

The season started on 16 August and ended on 1 October. The 16 August entry notes: 'Killed a number of old cocks; Saw a great many deer.' On the 21st: 'saw about fifty deer.' On the 23rd the first deer shot is recorded without comment. On the 25th: 'Saw 3 deer but no shot.' On the 28th: 'Unlucky. I saw about 120 deer: 16 stone; 11 points.' On the 31st: 'The wind changed and spoiled our chances; saw a great many.' On 3 September: 'Weight 13 st 3 lbs: 10 points.' On the 6th: 'Weight 10 st. 11lbs: 6 pts.' On the 7th: 'Wind changed and spoilt our chances: saw a great many;'... Total for the season was 415 head, which included 206 grouse and salmon as well as 11 deer, including what appears to have been a good royal. The emphasis had now largely switched from grouse shooting to stalking and some good beasts had been recorded.

1850

The year starting on 12 August and ending on 3 October reflects a similar continuing bias towards deer stalking....The total bag for the year was 505 head; 266 grouse; 134 hares; 15 salmon; 5 roe deer and 16 red deer. The deer by this time were becoming the important feature of the sport and to judge by the laconic comments some of the stags, including three royals and a fourteen-pointer, were of a very high standard.

The history of this area is typical of many in the Highlands. Once quite well populated in the 1780s, the ground was then cleared for sheep. In 1839 these in turn were removed for sporting purposes and within a decade it had been turned into a deer forest. Similar far-reaching changes were taking place throughout the Highlands. As the muzzle-loader gave way to the breech-loader in the 1860s and '70s and as smokeless powder was introduced during the 1870s and '80s the numbers of deer killed must have increased considerably. It is clear from these records, as well as from the early books on the subject, how many must have been wounded before it became possible to take a second shot without having the beast obscured by a cloud of black powder smoke.

In Britain at this period (mid-nineteenth century) sport was still changing rapidly. By 1836 the railways had begun to spread throughout the country and soon a network of lines was to proliferate everywhere. The net result was to open great areas of hitherto isolated country to the sportsman. The more enterprising began to look towards the Highlands of Scotland.

The game itself in some respects was being seriously affected. The last bustard was shot in the brecklands of East Anglia in 1838. By way of contrast in 1837 Sir Fowell Buxton in Norfolk, acting in conjunction with the famous naturalist

Llewellyn Lloyd in Sweden and the Marquis of Breadalbane in Scotland at Taymouth, succeeded in reintroducing the capercailie into Scotland.

In 1841 Hawker complained characteristically in his diaries about the lack of partridges as follows;

September 1st. The farmers it appears (in addition to mowing all the wheat stubbles and destroying for fuel all the turf banks where the birds could breed free from the rain and the scythe) have been using a solution of 1 lb of blue vitriol in a gallon of hot water to fortify each sack of sowing wheat from becoming smutty and most people think that many birds have been poisoned by feeding on this corn... So few birds seen (and those few so wild) that I got only six partridges. Expected vile sport, but nothing quite so execrable as this...

With the advent of the breech-loading shotgun in the 1850s, the whole sport of shooting was revolutionized. In the 1860s inevitably driven game shooting replaced the old method of walking up behind dogs. Instead of driving the birds into fields of roots and then walking them up in line or over dogs, the process was simply carried one stage further by driving the birds out of the roots again over the waiting guns. As might be expected there was some steadfast enthusiasts who kept to the old form of shooting over dogs, just as there were others who stood by the muzzle-loader, but each year their numbers grew less.

Admittedly there were some grounds for criticism of the early breech-loaders. They were heavier than the muzzle-loaders to start with and not as well balanced. Many of the early actions were not as strong as they should have been and when the gun was fired gaped dangerously at the breech, a defect which inevitably grew worse the more they were used. On the other hand there was no danger of an accidental burst through careless double-loading, or of an exploding powder-flask caused by smouldering powder in the barrels. The guns were much more easily cleaned and it was a simple matter to check whether mud or snow had been picked up which could result in a burst if the gun was fired with them blocked.

By 1866 the centre-fire hammer gun with various types of action had completely superseded the pin-fire guns. They were made with Damascus type barrels manufactured from alternate iron and steel bars twisted and coiled edge to edge round a steel mandril before being hammered into a solid welded cylinder. With butts of the best Circassian walnut and finely engraved actions, these guns were among the finer examples of the gunmaker's art. By this time English guns were famed throughout the world. Such names as Purdey, Lang, Lancaster, Boss, Dickson, Greener, Rigby, Holland and Holland, Webley and Scott were all famous then and are still well-known even today.

The next gunmaking advance was the manufacture of choked barrels whereby at last, after centuries of experiment, a gun could be made to shoot an open or closed pattern as required. Choke boring was first successfully produced by W.W. Greener in 1874. There followed merely the invention of the hammerless ejector in 1875 and from the 1880s onwards there was very little change in gun manufacture. The side-by-side double-barrelled shotgun with steel barrels remains in almost every detail exactly as it was then developed.

One of the important sportsmen who covered this transitional period between the muzzle-loader and the breech-loader was Sir Samuel White Baker, explorer of the sources of the Nile and big-game hunter in both Africa and India. He started his career by founding a tea planting colony at Newera Eliya in Ceylon, where he subsequently wrote a book in 1852 entitled *With Rifle and Hound in Ceylon* giving an enthralling account of his exploits there. Included in this was an exceedingly close encounter with an elephant, when he was shooting with black powder and a muzzle-loading double-barrelled rifle he had designed himself.

His party had already bagged nine elephants and, as he wrote:

'I had one barrel still loaded and I was pushing my way through the tangled undergrowth towards the spot where the dead elephants lay together, when I suddenly heard Wallace shriek out: 'Look out, sir! Look out! — an elephant's coming!'

I turned round in a moment and close past Wallace from the very spot where the last dead elephant lay, came the very essence and incarnation of a 'rogue' elephant in full charge. His trunk was thrown high in the air, his ears were cocked, his tail stood erect above his back as a poker, and screaming exactly like the whistle of a railway engine, he rushed upon me through the high grass with a velocity that was perfectly wonderful. His eyes flashed as he came on and he had singled me out as his victim.

I have often been in dangerous positions, but I never felt so totally devoid of hope as I did in this instance. The tangled grass rendered retreat impossible. I had only one barrel loaded, and that was useless, as the upraised trunk protected his forehead. I felt myself doomed; the few thoughts that rush through men's minds in such hopeless positions flew through mine and I resolved to wait for him until he was close upon me before I fired, hoping that he might lower his trunk and expose his forehead.

He rushed along at the pace of a horse at full speed, in a few moments as the grass flew to right and left before him, he was close upon me, but still his trunk was raised and I would not fire. One second more and at this headlong pace he was within three feet of me; down slashed his trunk with the rapidity of a whip thong, and with a shrill scream of fury he was upon me.

I fired at that instant; but in the twinkling of an eye I was flying through the air like a ball from a bat. At the moment of firing I had jumped to the left, but he struck me with his tusk in full charge upon my right thigh and hurled me eight or ten paces from him. That very moment he stopped and turning round he beat the grass about with his trunk, and commenced a strict search for me. I heard him advancing close to the spot where I lay still as death, knowing that my last chance lay in concealment. I heard the grass rustling close to me; closer and closer he approached, and at length beat the grass with his trunk several times exactly above me. I held my breath momentarily expecting to find his ponderous foot upon me. Although I had not felt the sensation of fear while I stood opposed to him, I felt what I never wish to feel again while he was deliberately hunting me up. Fortunately I had reserved my fire until the rifle almost touched him, for the powder and smoke had nearly blinded him and had spoiled his acute power of scent. To my joy I heard the rustling of the grass grow fainter; again I heard it at a still greater distance, at length it was gone!

At that time I thought that half my bones were broken, as I was numbed from head to foot by the force of the blow. His charge can be compared to a blow from a railway engine going at twenty miles an hour.

Not expecting to be able to move, I crept to my hands and knees. To my delight there were no bones broken and with a feeling of thankfulness I stood erect. I with difficulty reached a stream of water near the spot, where I bathed my leg, but in a few minutes it swelled to the size of man's waist.

Despite this he was back hunting the herd two days later and killed four more, two with a right and left from his double rifle.

By the mid-nineteenth century the advances in gunmaking were also being matched by corresponding advances in the rearing and preservation of game. Increasingly large numbers of pheasants were being reared and gamekepers were becoming more skilled in the art of driving birds to the guns waiting outside the coverts to produce larger bags. This in turn was causing a certain amount of criticism, as the following passage written in 1856, by 'Stonehenge' in his *Manual of Rural Sports,* indicates:

It is for the purposes of the *battue* that pheasants are now reserved and preserved with all the formidable retinue of head-keepers, under-keepers, day-watchers and night-watchers. None but men of large means and in possession of extensive coverts, can indulge in this amusement, except by the invitation of those who have at their command these pleasant auxiliaries to sport; but in this instance power has been abused and instead of promoting sport it has totally destroyed it. No-one can deny the fitness of the pheasant for affording gratification to the good sportsman, if the bird is fairly found, put up, and shot; but as well might 'mobbing' a fox be called fox-hunting, as a *battue* be considered genuine pheasant shooting; and this I will endeavour to show by the following description of the amusement; — in the *battue* nothing short of hundreds, or if possible, thousands, of killed, to say nothing of wounded, will constitute a successful day. The pseudo-sportsman who should be tempted from his fireside and his *Times* after breakfast by anything short of five brace an hour to his gun would be strongly inclined to complain, and would think, if he did not say, that his presence had been obtained under false pretences. The mode usually adopted is as follows: — First, gather together eight or ten crack shots, who may, many of them, be in wheeled-chairs, or on shooting ponies, but should be capable of killing, without spoiling, this beautiful bird; then having breakfasted the party, proceed to post them at certain stations where the game must cross a piece of open ground commanded by the shooters' guns. Thus in wide coverts, the guns are arranged along the edges of the open springs, at about forty or fifty yards apart, so as to command every head of game which passes, whether pheasant or hare, or sometimes rabbits &c, each shooter having two or three guns, and a man to load them. As soon as they are posted, the beaters are sent to the other end of the portion of wood which is being driven, and they proceed to drive the game through it, often with the aid of a steady dog or two, but as often without any assistance. For some time nothing is heard but the men calling to each other to keep the line, or their taps on the trees &c, which may be distinguished at a long distance; presently a hare canters quietly out of the edge of the covert, and, putting up her head to observe what is going on, is knocked over, — as easy a shot as a farmyard cock tied to a tree. Next, perhaps, a rabbit shares the same fate; she, however, seldom waits to look about her, but goes at a flying pace, and is a fair mark for a good shot. By and by, another and another shot is heard, with the squeal of a hare or two following them; then the beaters may be distinguished approaching, and their blows and cries are very audible. Expectation is on tiptoe, every moment being the one at which the slaughter is supposed to be about to begin; suddenly a loud 'whirr-r-r' is heard, followed by the peculiar 'cock, cock, cock-cockle' of the cock pheasant, of which some one, two or three rise from the edge of the high wood to be as certainly brought down; as fast as one falls, another shares his fate, and in ten minutes, or less, the ground is covered with the slain. In many instances low nets are fixed along the edge of the old wood, which compel the pheasants to get off their legs and rise, as they are so very tame, and so much inclined to run, as to escape in that way without the nets. In this manner the whole of the pheasants in a portion of the wood, or a great part of them, that is all those which have neither doubled back, nor escaped the guns, are brought to the bag, and the keeper's retrievers are set to work, to recover those which are not artistically disposed of. As soon as this portion of the work is accomplished, another portion of the wood is driven in a similar way; and this is again repeated, till the whole of the preserves are exhausted, so till the sporting(?) propensities of the guests are fully gratified. Now, it will be observed, that in this description nothing has been said of finding the game, or of the use of the instinct of the dog, or of the gratification of the desire for exercise, or even of the benefits derived from it; on the contrary, the admirers of this sport are generally wholly ignorant of the art of finding game, or of the hunting of the dogs, or unwilling or incapable of using their legs; they only long for blood — which may really be said to form the positive, comparative, and superlative degrees of their ideas on the subject. There may be some excuse for the boy feeling gratification and pride in obtaining the mastery over a fine pheasant in this kind of butchery; but I could never see the grounds for these feelings in a full-grown man, with all his faculties about him...

James Forsyth was born in Scotland in 1838. After schooling in Scotland he gained an MA at Cambridge and went out to India in the late 1850s. He served with distinction under Sir Richard Temple, Chief Commissioner of the Central Provinces, as Conservator of Forests. It was in this post that he surveyed the entire area, making numerous marches of over a thousand miles, lasting months at a time, through totally unexplored country. A fluent linguist and a keen sportsman, as well as an energetic stalker, he was in the perfect position to take full advantage of the sport available.

His first book, published in 1862 was entitled *The Sporting Rifle and its Projectiles*. Although published at a time of great change in all forms of firearms there was clearly a considerable demand for it as in 1867 he published a much revised, though even then soon outdated, second edition. In the preface he wrote:

The progress of gunnery since the publication of the first edition has necessitated many additions to the present work. Most of it has been re-written and the plates are almost entirely new.

I trust the work will now be found to be a complete guide to the young sportsman in all matters connected with the SPORTING RIFLE.

He wrote at one point:

Baker [Sir Samuel White Baker] says, if I remember right, that a good shot should be able to bag *without fail*, everything fired at standing at seventy yards or running at fifty. I have never met a man yet who could bag *without fail* all animals at any distance. I think myself that if one fires at fair standing shots within 150 yards and running within 100 yards he should kill two out of three in the former case and one half of the latter.

He recommended:

'As a rule the place to hit all mammals is through the shoulders, the lungs or heart are thus penetrated and besides the bones of the shoulder may be broken and escape prevented...'

In the work for which he is better known, *The Highlands of Central India; Notes on Their Forests and Wild Tribes, Natural History and Sports*, the product of his many explorations, published in 1871, he wrote:

The labour of exploring such forests...during the hot season when alone they are sufficiently open and free from malaria, is immense — day after day toiling over these interminable basaltic ridges, where many marches are often to be made without meeting an inhabitant, without often a single green tree for shelter, and dependent for water on a few stagnant pools puddled up by the feet of wild animals. This was often what fell to the lot of the forest officers...and there is not one whose health did not after a few years give way under the combined assaults of malaria and a fiery sun...

On the subject of shooting the sambar deer, he pointed out that:

...if information can be got from the people who frequent the jungles for wood cutting, etc., of whereabouts the sambar are feeding and resting...capital sport can be got with them in the day time with the aid of a riding elephant. This enables you to see over the grass, and generally starts any sambar that may be lying down within about a hundred yards. The elephant must be thoroughly trained to stop dead short on deer getting up and should not be furnished with a

howdah, the simple pad or charjama being preferable for this sort of shooting; and the smaller and more active the elephant is the better... A standing shot may sometimes be had during the few seconds after the sambar first rise, but more generally they dart off at full speed at once and then comes into play the most difficult of all the arts of the rifleman — snap shooting at running game off an elephant. The elephant is never perfectly still for more than a moment and its short swing must be allowed for as well as the pace of the deer. The sambar is, of course, from its great size and distinct colour, much more easy to note than the spotted deer, or barking, or hog, deer, but still it is amazing what a preponderance of clean misses the best shots will make at even running sambar off the elephant, until long and constant practice has given the peculiar knack which is so difficult to attain. It is, however, by far the most deadly as well as one of the most enjoyable ways of hunting the sambar. Driving a large extent of country with a long line of beaters is the commonest method... It is frequently successful and often secures a good stag, but for my own part I have seldom resorted to it... The whole country is disturbed; the shooting of a creature driven up to you, without the exercise either of skill or any other manly quality on your own part is not sport...it has never been my fortune (not that I have much regretted it) to be out with a large hunting party in India....

By far the finest sport afforded by the sambar is when he is regularly stalked in his native wilderness, without either elephant or beaters. I will not waste a word on so vile a practice as that of shooting him at night, when he comes to the crops or drinking places. None but a native shikar, or a European with equally poaching proclivities would ever think of such a thing...

Forsyth was never afraid to speak of his misses and disasters, a sure sign of a thoroughgoing sportsman, who knows that such things must often occur to everyone. On one occasion he wrote:

Just as we arrived some dogs passed...in full cry after a doe sambar they had roused. Of course we flew to our rifles, but were just in time to miss her handsomely as she dashed into the thick jungle... On another occasion after walking several miles along the backbone of the ridge beyond Bingara...I caught the glint of the sun on something moving, and made out a noble sambar stag... He was not more than a mile off in a direct line; but to get to the spot it would be necessary to go several miles round the head of a small ravine... We carefully marked the spot, and...started off at a brisk walk to circumvent him. The sun was well up by now and it is very hot in March even at that early hour... At last we sighted the red topped tree under which we had marked our stag... We were not to succeed however...the Bheel (his native attendant) accidentally stepped on a leaf and the game was up. Though I dashed ahead at once...all I saw was a dark form running low, but at a great pace...too far off for a shot.

Forsyth commented:

No-one can hunt in these scantily covered hills without wondering at the extreme difficulty of making out such large animals as sambar, bison and bears on the open hillside. The bison and bear perfectly resemble the large black trap boulders that thickly strew every hill; and thus the glaring contrast of their black hides with the bright yellow grass frequently attracts no attention whatever...

He recorded on another occasion:

...something caught my eye... It looked exactly like one of the bunches of twigs that grow out of old teak stumps with one or two dried leaves attached to them; and yet I fancied that I had seen it move. I looked at it intently for at least a minute, trying to make out if it was a bunch of teak twigs or a sambar's head and horns. It never moved in the whole of this time; and as the Bheels who were with me said it was only a stump, I turned to pass on. The glint of my rifle barrel must have caught in the sun, for a noble stag started from his lair...wheeled round and clattered away. My hasty shot missed him clean...and I turned for home swearing to expend a bullet in future on every teak stump that bore the most distant resemblance to a stag's head. Both T. [his companion] and I were often mistaken in these hills in the same manner and have frequently gone up to within a few yards of a stump to make sure. The resemblance is very close...Even the motion of the huge ears of the sambar, which they restrain only in the presence of danger, answers exactly to the stirring of a dried teak leaf in a slight breeze...

Forsyth described a gruelling hot day's hunt after a herd of bison with a friend when eventually:

...I ran up to T. in time to see ten or twelve bison scrambling up the opposite side of the ravine. A bull brought up the rear...so we opened fire...and the third shot broke his leg. He had the other shots too, and, after limping on a bit, staggered, and fell down the hill. Being much fatigued by the heat of a very sultry April day, we waited there till the people came up with our leathern water-sack to have a drink and then went over to the bull, who was still alive, but unable to rise...

The following day they shot a sambar and another bison. Forsyth made the point that:

It is easy to throw in half a dozen bull bison in a day's sport by the stroke of a pen... I have however stuck to the exact facts of a by no means heavy bag, on purpose to give a more accurate idea of what such shooting really means — namely very hard work and much exposure for an average of certainly no more than one head of game a day — and often much less...

Adding that:

By taking every chance of cow bison and doe sambar of course the bag could be greatly increased; and I heard of two men who in the course of one year murdered in this way twenty-eight bison in one week. This is not sport, nor are the performers sportsmen. The bison is already, it would seem, diminishing in numbers... He is one of the most harmless animals to the industry of man, and, fairly hunted, affords perhaps the best sport in India; it would be a pity, then, if his numbers should be unduly diminished by unsportsmanlike conduct.

There were still sportsmen in his native Scotland whom James Forsyth would have appreciated. Charles St John, whose *Wild Sports and Natural History of the Highlands,* which ran into nine editions before the turn of the century, was one such. His description of his chase after the Muckle Hart of Benmore is a classic of its kind:

Sunday — This evening, Malcolm, the shepherd of the shealing at the foot of Benmore, returning from church, reported his having crossed on the hill a track of a hart of extraordinary size and he guessed it must be 'the muckle stag of Benmore'. This was an animal seldom seen, but which had long been the talk and marvel of the shepherds for its wonderful size and cunning. They love the marvellous and in their report 'the muckle stag' bore a charmed life; he was unapproachable and invulnerable. I had heard of him too and having got the necessary information, resolved to try and break the charm, though it should cost me a day or two.

Monday — This morning at sunrise, I with my rifle, Donald carrying my old double-barrel, and Bran, took our way up the glen to the shealing at the foot of Benmore. Donald had no heart for this expedition. He is not addicted to superfluous conversation, but I heard him mutter something of a 'feckless errand — as good deer nearer hame.' Bran had already been the victor in many a bloody tussle with hart and fox. We held for the most part up the glen, but turning and crossing to seek every likely corrie and burn on both sides. I shot a wild cat stealing home to its cairn in the early morning; and we several times in the day came on deer, but they were hinds with their calves and I was bent on higher game. As night fell we turned down to the shealing rather disheartened; but the shepherd cheered me by assuring me the hart was still in that district, and by describing his track, which he said was like that of a good-sized heifer. Our spirits were quite restored by a meal of fresh-caught trout, oatcake and milk, with a modicum of whisky, which certainly was of unusual flavour and potency.

Tuesday — We were off again by daybreak. I will pass by several minor adventures, but one cannot be omitted. Malcolm went with us to show us where he had last seen the track. As we crossed a long reach of black and broken ground, the first ascent from the valley, two golden eagles rose out of a hollow at some distance. Their flight was lazy and heavy, as if gorged with food, and on examining the place we found the carcass of a sheep half-eaten, one of Malcolm's flock. He vowed vengeance; and, merely pointing out to us our route, returned for a spade to dig a place of hiding near enough to the carcass to enable him to have a shot at the eagles if they should return. We held on our way, and the greater part of the day without any luck to cheer us, my resolution 'not to be beat' being, however, a good deal strengthened by the occasional grumbling of Donald. Towards the afternoon, when we had tired ourselves with looking with our glasses at every corrie in that side of the hill, at length, in crossing a bare and boggy patch of ground, Donald suddenly stopped with a Gaelic exclamation, and pointed — and there, to be sure, was a full fresh imprint, the largest mark of deer either of us had ever seen. There was no more grumbling. Both of us were instantly as much on the alert as when we started on our adventure. We traced the track as long as the ground would allow.

Where we lost it, it seemed to point down the little burn, which soon lost itself to our view in a gorge of bare rocks. We proceeded now very cautiously, and taking up our station on a concealed ledge of one of the rocks, began to search the valley below with our telescopes. It was a large flat, strewed with huge slabs of stone, and surrounded on all sides but one with dark rocks. At the further end were two black lochs, connected by a sluggish stream; beside the larger loch a bit of coarse grass and rushes, where we could distinguish a brood of wild ducks swimming in and out. It was difficult ground to see a deer in, if lying; and I had almost given up seeking, when Donald's glass became motionless, and he gave a sort of grunt as he changed his posture, but without taking his glass from his eye. 'Ugh! I'm thinking yon's him, sir. I'm seeing his horns.' I was at first incredulous. What he showed me close to the long grass I have mentioned looked for all the world like some withered sticks; but the doubt was short. While we gazed the stag rose and commenced feeding; and at last I saw the great hart of Benmore! He was a long way off, perhaps a mile and a half, but in excellent ground for getting at him. Our plan was soon arranged. I was to stalk him with the rifle, while Donald with my gun and Bran, was to get round, out of sight, to the pass, by which the deer was likely to leave the valley. My task was apparently very easy. After getting down behind the rock I had scarcely to stoop my head, but to walk up within shot, so favourable was the ground and the wind. I walked cautiously, however, and slowly, to give Donald time to reach the pass. I was now within three hundred yards of him, when, as I leant against a slab of stone, all hid below my eyes, I saw him give a sudden start, stop feeding, and look around suspiciously. What a noble beast! what a stretch of antler! with a mane like a lion! He stood for a minute or two, snuffing every breath. I could not guess the cause of his alarm; it was not myself — the light wind blew fair down from him upon me; and I knew Donald would give him no inkling of his whereabouts. He presently began to move, and came at a slow trot directly towards me. My pulse beat high. Another hundred yards forward and he is mine! But it was not so to be. He took the top of a steep bank which commanded my position, saw me in an instant, and was off, at the speed of twenty miles an hour, to a pass wide from that where Donald was hid. While clattering up the hill, scattering the loose stones behind him, two other stags joined him, which had evidently been put up by Donald, and had given the alarm to my quarry. It was then that his great size was conspicuous, I could see with my glass that they were full-grown stags, and with good heads, but they looked like fallow-deer as they followed him up the crag. I sat down, disappointed for the moment, and Donald soon joined me, much crestfallen and cursing the stag in a curious variety of Gaelic oaths. Still it was something to have seen 'the muckle stag' and *nil desperandum* was my motto. We had a long and weary walk to Malcolm's shealing; and I was glad to get to my heather bed, after arranging that I should occupy the hiding-place Malcolm had prepared near the dead sheep next morning,

Wednesday — We were up an hour before daylight; and in a very dark morning I sallied out with Malcolm to take my station for a shot at the eagles. Many a stumble and slip I made during our walk, but at last I was left alone fairly ensconced in the hiding-place, which gave me hardly room to stand, sit, or lie. My position was not very comfortable, and the air was nipping cold just before the break of day. It was scarcely grey dawn when a bird with a slow flapping flight, passed the opening of my hut, and lighted out of sight, but near, for I heard him strike the ground; and my heart beat faster. What was my disappointment when his low crowing croak announced the raven! and presently he came in sight, hopping and walking suspiciously round the sheep; till, supposing the coast clear, and little wotting of the double-barrel, he hopped upon the carcass, and began with his square cut-and-thrust beak to dig at the meat. Another raven soon joined him, and then two more; who after a kind of parley, quite intelligible, though in an unknown tongue, were admitted to their share of the banquet. I was watching their voracious meal with interest, when suddenly they set up a croak of alarm, stopped feeding, and all turned their knowing-eyes in one direction. At that moment I heard a sharp scream, but very distant. The black party heard it too; and instantly darted off, alighting again at a little distance. Next moment a rushing noise, and a large body passed close to me; and the monarch of the clouds alighted at once on the sheep, with his broad breast not fifteen yards from me. He quietly folded up his wings; and throwing back his magnificent head, looked round at the ravens, as if wondering at their impudence in approaching his breakfast table. They kept a respectful silence and hopped a little farther off. The royal bird then turned his head in my direction, attracted by the alteration in the appearance of the ground which he had just noticed in the dim morning light. His bright eye that instant caught mine as it glanced along the barrel. He rose; as he did so I drew the trigger, and he fell quite dead half a dozen yards from the sheep. I followed Malcolm's directions, who had predicted that one eagle would be followed by a second, and remained quiet, in hope that his mate was not within hearing of my shot. The morning was brightening and I had not waited many minutes when I saw the other eagle skimming low over the brow of the hill towards me. She did not alight at once. Her eye caught the change in the ground or the dead body of her mate, and she wheeled up into the air. I thought her lost to me, when presently I heard her wings brush close over my head; and then she went wheeling round and round above the dead bird, and turning her head downwards to make out what had happened. At times she stooped so low I could see the sparkle of her eye and hear her low complaining cry. I watched the time when she turned up her wing towards me and fired, and dropped her actually on the body of the other. I now rushed out. The last bird immediately rose to her feet and stood gazing at me with a reproachful, half-threatening look. She would have done battle, but death was busy with her; and as I was loading in haste, she reeled and fell perfectly dead. Eager as I had been to do the deed, I could not look on the royal birds without a pang. But such regrets were now too late. Passing over the shepherd's rejoicing and my incredible breakfast, I must return to our great adventure. Our line of march today was over ground so high that we came repeatedly into the midst of ptarmigan. On the very summit, Bran had a rencontre with an old mountain fox, toothless, yet very fat, whom he made to bite the dust. We struck at one place the tracks of the three deer, but of the animals themselves we saw nothing. We kept exploring corrie after corrie till night fell; and as it was in vain to think of returning to the shealing, which yet was the nearest roof, we were content to find a sort of niche in the rock, tolerably screened from all winds; and having almost filled it with long heather, flower upwards, we wrapped our plaids around us, and slept pretty comfortably.

Thursday — A dip in the burn below our bivouac renovated me. I did not observe that Donald followed my example in that; but he joined me in a hearty attack on the viands which still remained in our bag; and we started with renewed courage. About mid-day we came on a shealing beside a long narrow loch, fringed with beautiful weeping-birches, and there we found means to cook some grouse which I had shot to supply our exhausted larder. The shepherd who had 'no Sassenach' cheered us by his report of 'the deer' being lately seen, and describing his usual haunts. Donald was plainly getting disgusted and home-sick. For myself, I looked upon it as my fate that I must have that hart; so on we trudged. Repeatedly that afternoon we came on the fresh tracks of our chase, but still he remained invisible. As it got dark, the weather suddenly changed, and I was glad to let Donald seek for the bearings of a 'whisky bothie' which he had heard of at our last stopping-place. While he was seeking for it the rain began to fall heavily, and through the darkness we were just able to distinguish a dark object, which turned out be a horse. 'The lads with the still will no be far off,' said Donald. And so it turned out. But the rain had increased the darkness so much, that we should have searched in vain if I had not distinguished at intervals, between the pelting of the rain and the heavy rushing of the black burn that ran beside us, what appeared to me to be the shrill treble of a fiddle. I could scarcely believe my ears. But when I communicated the intelligence to Donald, whose ears were less acute, he jumped with joy. 'It's all right enough, sir; just follow the sound; it's that drunken deevil, Sandy Ross; ye'll never haud a fiddle frae him, nor him frae a whisky-still.' It was clear the sound came from across the black stream, and it looked formidable in the dark. However, there was no remedy. So grasping each other's collars, and holding our guns high over head, we dashed in, and staggered through in safety, though the water was up to my waist, running like a mill-race, and the bottom was of round slippery stones. Scrambling up the bank, and following the merry sound, we came to what seemed a mere hole in the bank, from which it proceeded. The hole was partially closed by a door woven of heather; and looking through it we saw a sight worthy of Teniers. On a barrel in the middle of the apartment — half hut, half cavern — stood aloft, fiddling with all his might, the identical Sandy Ross, while round him danced three unkempt savages; and another figure was stooping, employed over a fire in the corner, where the whisky-pot was in full operation. The fire, and a sliver or two of lighted bog-fir, gave light enough to see the whole, for the place was not above ten feet square. We made our approaches with becoming caution, and were, it is needless to say, hospitably received; for who ever heard of Highland smugglers refusing a welcome to sportsmen? We got rest, food and fire — all that we had required — and something more; for long after I had betaken me to the dry heather in the corner, I had disturbed visions of strange orgies in the bothie, and of my sober Donald exhibiting curious antics on the top of a tub. These might have been the productions of a disturbed brain; but there is no doubt that when daylight awoke me, the smugglers and Donald were all quiet and asleep, far past my efforts to rouse them, with the exception

of one who was still able to tend the fire under the large black pot.

Friday — From the state in which my trusty companion was, with his head in a heap of ashes, I saw it would serve no purpose to wake him, even if I were able to do so. It was quite clear he would be good for nothing all day. I therefore secured some breakfast and provisions for the day (part of them oatcake, which I baked for myself) tied up Bran to wait Donald's restoration, and departed with my rifle alone. The morning was bright and beautiful, the mountain-streams overflowing with last night's rain. I was now thrown on my own resources, and my own knowledge of the country, which, to say the truth, was far from minute, or exact. 'Benna-skiach' was my object to-day, and the corries which lay beyond it, where at this season the large harts were said to resort. My way at first was dreary enough, over a long slope of boggy ground, enlivened, however, by a few traces of deer having crossed, though none of my 'chase.' I at length passed the slope, and soon topped the ridge, and was repaid for my labour by a view so beautiful that I sat down to gaze at it, though anxious to get forward. Looking down into the valley before me, the foreground was a confusion of rocks of most fantastic shape, shelving rapidly to the edge of a small blue lake, the opposite shore of which was a beach of white pebbles, and beyond, a stretch of the greenest pasture, dotted with drooping white-stemmed birches. This little level was hemmed in on all sides by mountains, ridge above ridge, the lowest closely covered with purple heath, the next more green and broken by ravines, and the highest ending in sharp serrated peaks tipped with snow. Nothing moved within range of my vision, and nothing was to be seen that bespoke of life but a solitary heron standing on one leg in the shallow water at the upper end of the lake. From hence I took in a good range, but could see no deer. While I lay above the lake, the day suddenly changed, and heavy wraiths of mist came down the mountain-sides in rapid succession. They reached me soon and I was enclosed in an atmosphere through which I could not see twenty yards. It was very cold, too, and I was obliged to move, though scarcely knowing whither. I followed the course of the lake, and afterwards of the stream which flowed from it, for some time. Now and then a grouse would rise close to me, and, flying a few yards, alight again on a hillock, crowing and croaking at the intruder. The heron, in the darkness, came flapping his great wings close past me; I almost fancied I could feel the movement they caused in the air. Nothing could be done in such weather, and I was not sure I might not be going away from my object. It was getting late too, and I made up my mind that my most prudent plan was to arrange a bivouac before it became quite dark. My wallet was empty, except a few crumbs, the remains of my morning's baking. It was necessary to provide food; and just as the necessity occurred to me, I heard, through the mist, the call of a cock grouse as he alighted close to me. I contrived to get his head between me and the sky as he was strutting and croaking on a hillock close at hand; and aiming at where his body ought to be, I fired my rifle. On going up to the place, I found I had not only killed him, but also his mate, whom I had not seen. It was a commencement of good luck. Sitting down, I speedily skinned my birds, and took them down to the burn to wash them before cooking. In crossing a sandy spot beside the burn, I came upon — could I believe my eyes? — 'the Track'. Like Robinson Crusoe in similar circumstances, I started back; but was speedily at work taking my information. There were prints enough to show that the hart had crossed at a walk leisurely. It must have been lately, for it was since the burn had returned to its natural size, after the last night's flood. But nothing could be done till morning, so I set about my cooking; and having after some time succeeded in lighting a fire, while my grouse were slowly broiling, I pulled a quantity of heather, which I spread in a corner a little protected by an overhanging rock; I spread my plaid upon it and over the plaid built another layer of heather. My supper ended, which was not epicurean, I crawled into my nest under my plaid, and was soon sound asleep. I cannot say that my slumbers were unbroken. I dreamt of the great stag thundering up the hills with preternatural speed, and of noises like cannon (which I have since learnt to attribute to their cause — the splitting of fragments of rock under a sudden change from wet to sharp frost), and above all, the constant recurrence of visions of weary struggles through fields of snow and ice kept me restless; and at length awoke me to the consciousness of a brilliant skylight and keen frost — a change that rejoiced me in spite of the cold.

Saturday — Need I say my first object was to go down and examine the track anew. There was no mistake. It was impossible to doubt that 'the muckle hart of Benmore'; had actually walked through that burn a few hours before me, and in the same direction. I followed the track and breasted the opposite hill. Looking round from its summit, it appeared to me a familiar scene, and on considering a moment, I found I overlooked from a different quarter the very same rocky plain and the two black lochs where I had seen my chase three days before. I had not gazed many minutes when I saw a deer lying on a black hillock which was quite open. I lay down immediately, and with my glass made out at once the object of all my wanderings. My joy was somewhat abated by his position, which was not easily approachable. My first object, however, was to withdraw myself out of his sight, which I did by crawling backwards down a little bank till only the tops of his horns were visible, and they served to show me that he continued still. As he lay looking towards me, he commanded with his eye three-fourths of the circle, and the other quarter where one might have got in upon him under cover of the little hillock, was unsafe from the wind blowing in that direction. A burn ran between him and me, one turn of which seemed to come within two hundred yards of him. It was my only chance; so, retreating about half a mile, I got into the burn in hidden ground, and then crept up its channel with such caution that I never allowed myself a sight of more than the tips of his horns, till I had reached the nearest bend to him. There, looking through a tuft of rushes, I had a perfect view of the noble animal, lying upon the open hillock, lazily stretched out at length, and only moving now and then to scratch his flank with his horn. I watched him for fully an hour, the water up to my knees all the time. At length he stirred, gathered his legs together, and rose; and arching his back, he stretched himself just as a bullock does when rising from his night's lair. My heart throbbed, as turning all round he seemed to try the wind for his security, and then walked straight to the burn, at a point about a hundred and fifty yards from me. I was much tempted, but had resolution to reserve my fire, reflecting that I had but one barrel. He went into the burn at a deep pool, and standing in it up to his knees, took a long drink. I stooped to put on a new copper cap and prick the nipple of my rifle; and — on looking up again, he was gone! I was in despair; and was on the point of moving rashly, when I saw his horns again appear a little further off, but not more than fifty yards from the burn. By and by they lowered, and I judged he was lying down. 'You are mine at last,' I said; and I crept cautiously up the bed of the burn till I was opposite where he had lain down. I carefully and inch by inch placed my rifle over the bank, and then ventured to look along it. I could see only his horns, but within an easy shot. I was afraid to move higher up the bed of the burn, where I could have seen his body; the direction of the wind made that dangerous. I took breath for a moment, and screwed up my nerves; and then with my cocked rifle at my shoulder and my finger on the trigger, I kicked a stone, which splashed into the water. He started up instantly; but exposed only his front towards me. Still he was very near, scarcely fifty yards, and I fired at his throat just where it joins the head. He dropped on his knees to my shot; but was up again in a moment, and went staggering up the hill. Oh, for one hour of Bran! Although he kept on at a mad pace, I saw he was becoming too weak for the hill. He swerved and turned back to the burn; and came headlong down within ten yards of me, tumbling into it apparently dead. Feeling confident, from the place where my ball had taken effect, that he was dead, I threw down my rifle, and went up to him with my hunting-knife. I found him stretched out, and as I thought dying; and I laid hold of his horns to raise his head to bleed him. I had scarcely touched him when he sprang up, flinging me backwards on the stones. It was an awkward position. I was stunned by the violent fall; behind me was a steep bank seven or eight feet high; before me the bleeding stag with his horns levelled at me, and cutting me off from my rifle. In desperation I moved; when he instantly charged, but fortunately tumbled ere he quite reached me. He drew back again like a ram about to butt, and then stood still with his head lowered, and his eyes bloody and swelled, glaring upon me. His mane and all his coat were dripping with water and blood; and as he now and then tossed his head with an angry snort, he looked like some savage beast of prey. We stood mutually at bay for some time, till recovering myself, I jumped out of the burn so suddenly, that he had not time to run at me, and from the bank above, I dashed my plaid over his head and eyes, and threw myself upon him. I cannot account for my folly, and it had nearly cost me dear. The poor beast struggled desperately, and his remaining strength foiled me in every attempt to stab him in front; and he at length made off, tumbling me down, but carrying with him a stab in the leg which lamed him. I ran and picked up my rifle, and then kept him in view as he rushed down the burn on three legs towards the loch. He took the water and stood at bay up to his chest in it. As soon as he halted, I commenced loading my rifle, when to my dismay I found that all the balls I had remaining were for my double-barrel and were a size too large for my rifle. I sat down and commenced scraping one to the right size, an operation that seemed interminable. At last I succeeded; and having loaded, the poor stag remaining perfectly still, I went up within twenty yards of him, and shot him through the head. He turned over and floated, perfectly dead.

I waded in and towed him ashore, and then had leisure to look at my wounds and bruises, which were not serious, except my shin-bone, which was scraped from ankle to knee by his horn. I soon had cleaned my quarry and stowed him away as safely as I could, and then turned down the glen at a gay pace. I found Donald with Bran reposing at Malcolm's shealing; and for all reproaches on his misconduct, I was satisfied with sending him to bring home 'the muckle hart of Benmore,' a duty which he performed before night fall.

Inevitably, during his many years in India, Forsyth did not restrict himself entirely to Sambar and bison. He also took the opportunity when available to shoot tigers and panthers. He was an enthusiast in every sense of the word and was amongst the first to advocate travelling to India for sporting purposes. He wrote:

While wandering about in 1862, during the months of April and May in the teak forests of the Betul district, I devoted a day now and then to the sport of tiger shooting; and it was the laudable custom of the forest officers to spare if possible every year, a few weeks during the height of the hot season for the purpose of making an impression on the numerous tigers which at that time rendered working in the forests and carrying timber so dreaded by the natives and consequently costly to the Government.

Although there is much in the sport of tiger-hunting that renders it inferior as a mere exercise, or as an effort of skill, to some other sports of these regions (for many a man has bagged his forty or fifty tigers who has never succeeded in bagging by fair stalking, a single bull bison or stag sambar) yet there is a stirring of the blood in attacking an animal before whom every other beast of the forest quails, and unarmed man is helpless as the mouse under the paw of the cat...which draws men to its continued pursuit after that of every other animal has ceased to afford sufficient excitement to undergo the toil of hunting in a tropical country.

...the hot season, the height of which is in April and May, is the most favourable time for hunting the tiger. Then the water supply...is at its lowest...and the tiger...seeks the lowest valleys, where...much of the game he preys on has congregated...

Forsyth commented that two types of tiger were generally recognized by the native shikaris. One, which lived on game alone chiefly in the hills was very innocuous, even beneficial in keeping down the herds of deer, which otherwise might have attacked the crops. The other was an older, heavier animal which preyed on cattle. Forsyth argued that in reality the game-killing tiger merely graduated as it grew older onto killing cattle, growing heavier and lazier as a result.He noted, however, that:

'It is useless to devote much time to hunting the hill tigers which prey on game alone. They are so scattered over extensive tracts of jungle and are so active and wary that it is only by accident that they are ever brought to the bag.' He continued: 'Favourably situated covers are almost certain to hold one or more cattle-eating tigers during the hot weather; and, however many are killed, others will shortly occupy their place...'

He also pointed out:

The tiger very seldom kills his prey by the 'sledge hammer stroke' of his forepaws so often talked about, the usual way being to seize with the teeth by the nape of the neck and at the same time use the paws to hold the victim, and give a purchase for the wrench that dislocates the neck...

Tigers that prey on cattle are generally perfectly well-known to the cowherds. The damage that they do on the whole is very great, sixty or seventy head of cattle...being destroyed in...a year. Generally there is...one native...whose profession is that of shikari, or hunter... When he hears of a bullock having been killed...erecting a platform...in the nearest tree...[he] watches by night for the return of the tiger... His weapon is a long matchlock, which he loads with six 'fingers' of powder and two bullets. These fly a little apart and if they hit are usually the death of the tiger. His method of shooting is sometimes imitated by lazy European sportsmen.

Following the lead of Walter Campbell [an earlier Indian sportsman and Scot] he argued:

The best way of hunting the tiger is undoubtedly...to bring in the aid of the trained elephant and to follow and shoot him in his mid-day retreat... No sort of hunting requires more careful arrangements, greater knowledge of the animal, perseverance and good shooting, than the pursuit of the tiger by a single sportsman with a single elephant... Some people affect to despise...using elephants...and talk a great deal about shooting them on foot. As regards danger to the sportsman, nine tenths of the tigers said to be shot on foot are really killed from trees, or rocks, where the sportsman is quite secure. The only danger then is to the unfortunate beaters, if used... In this method of hunting many more tigers are wounded than secured, the only danger lying in following up a wounded animal, which is usually avoided and thus an innocent animal is often converted into the scourge of the countryside. A very few sportsmen do for a short period of their lives, make a practice of hunting and shooting tigers really on foot; but they are seldom very successful and sooner or later get killed, or have such narrow escapes as to cure them of such silly folly for the rest of their days. A man on foot has no chance whatever in thick jungle with a tiger that is bent on killing him. He cannot see a yard before him and is himself conspicuous to every sense of the brute...who can move at will through the thickest cover without the slightest sound or stir... The sportsman who as a rule uses an elephant in thick cover will find quite enough opportunities...of testing his nerve on foot, particularly if he tracks his own game instead of employing shikaris to do so... Much of the excitement of the sport depends on the...method of attacking the tiger. As a rule when an elephant is on fair ground the object should be to get the tiger to charge instead of allowing him to sneak away...

With an acute understanding of the native mind Forsyth wrote:

A great many reasons...combine to make the natives...very unwilling to give information about tigers. Firstly it is liable to bring down a large encampment of 'Sahibs' on their village, which they, very justly in most cases, dislike. The military officer who scorns to learn the rural language and his train of overbearing, swindling servants...stinks in the nostrils of the poor inhabitants of the tracts where tigers are found. The tiger himself is in fact far more endurable [and] they fear that they will be made to beat for the tiger...with a considerable chance of getting killed and very little of being paid... On the other hand a properly organised expedition, where the sportsman provides his own supplies and his means of hunting is certain to meet with every co-operation from the people. They will even crowd in to help driving the jungles, when they know they are to work for a good sportsman and shot who will not unnecessarily risk their lives.

Forsyth was responsible for organising a tiger hunt for the Governor-General of India in January 1861, when a royal tiger was secured. In recording the event he wrote that he:

...mounted sentry over that beast for nearly a week, girding him in a little hill with a belt of fires and feeding him with nightly kine, till half a hundred elephants carrying the cream of the vice-regal camp swept him out into the plain, where he fell riddled by a storm of bullets from several hundred virgin rifles. He had the honour of being painted by Landseer, by the blaze of torchlight, under the shadow of the British standard; and my howdah bore witness, of many a day, in a bullet hole through both sides of it, to the accuracy of aim of some gallant member of the staff.

Forsyth was clear about tiger hunting:

...having discovered a tract where tigers are reported, a good central place should be selected for a camp...near a village... The sportsman will probably find...the village headman...waiting to receive him with a simple offering — a pot of milk, or a bunch of plantains... If he is welcome tales will not be wanting of the neighbouring tigers...The usual haunts of the tiger will be described... The shikari of the neighbourhood will be present or can be sent for... Rupees, or the prospect of them, will be wanted to loosen his tongue...if you are known to be a good paymaster he will willingly serve you. In my earlier sporting days I always went out to make the preliminary exploration for tigers myself; and this is the only way to learn the business thoroughly, so as to be able afterwards to devolve the labour on your shikaris. A sportsman who is not thoroughly master of this business will never have a reliable shikari... The morning is the best time for this work. It is then cool and every footprint of the previous night is sharp and clear... The movements of the tiger even may often be traced up to eight or nine o'clock by the voices of monkeys and peafowl, the chatter of crows and small birds and the bark of sambar and spotted deer. The whole nocturnal life of the beasts of the forest is then displayed in the clearest manner to the hunter whose eye has been trained to read this book of nature... Everywhere the cruel tyranny of the tiger has imprinted itself on the faithful page. His track to the water is straight and leisurely, while that of the nilgar or spotted deer is halting and suspicious and apt to end in a wild scurry to right or left when it crosses the tiger's. Here and there bleaching skulls and bones show that the whole herd have not always made good their escape...not seldom the trampled soil and traces of blood and hair show where a stubborn boar has successfully resisted the attack of a tiger. Bruin alone is tolerably safe from the assault of the tiger; but he too gets out of this way like the rest and drinks at a different pool...

On another occasion Forsyth:

...followed a tiger in the early morning for several miles up the bed of a stream entirely by the demonstrations of the large Hanuman monkeys, of which there were numbers feeding on the wild fruits... Each group continued to swear at him till he had passed out of sight... The river took a broad sweep...and by cutting across the neck I managed to arrive...in front of the tiger... He was travelling under the opposite bank (and) passed within twenty yards of me, making for a small ravine... I let him get to the mouth of the ravine before I fired...and on receiving the shot he bounded forward into its cover... I knew he was hit to death...but we then went round a good way to where a high bank overlooked the ravine into which he had disappeared. Here we cautiously peered over...and found the tiger lying stone dead shot near the heart.

In 1865 he shot a cattle-eating tiger which was reputed to have killed over a thousand head and forced the natives to abandon one of the best grazing areas available. Forsyth wrote:

He was a very large tiger, measuring ten feet one inch in length as he lay and was a perfect mountain of fat — the fat of a thousand kine as the cowherds lugubriously remarked...ten feet one inch is the length of an unusually large tiger. The average length from nose to tip of the tail is only nine feet six inches for a full grown male and for a tigress about eight feet four inches. The experience of all sportsmen I have met with whose accuracy I could rely on is the same... The skin of a ten-foot tiger will easily stretch to thirteen or fourteen feet if required...A well-known sportsman and writer, whose recorded measurements have done more to extend the size of the tiger than anything else informed me that all his measurements were taken from flat skins...the British public demands twelve-foot tigers, just as it refuses to accept an Indian landscape without palm trees...

Forsyth continued:

A strange affection springs up between the hunter and his well-tried ally in the chase of a tiger... No one who has not witnessed it would believe the astonishing caution with which a well-trained elephant approaches a tiger — removing with noiseless adroitness every obstacle of fallen timber etc., and passing his huge bulk over rustling leaves, or rolling stones, or quaking bog with an absolute and marvelous silence: handing up stones, when ordered, for his master to fling into the cover; smelling out a cold scent as a spaniel rodes a pheasant; and at last, perhaps, pointing dead with a sensitive trunk at the hidden monster, or showing with short nervous raps of that organ on the ground that he is somewhere near, though not actually discovered to the senses of the elephant... The elephant's business is to stand like a rock in every event, even when the tiger is fastened on his head — as many a good one has done and will do...

Discussing what was desirable in a good hunting elephant he wrote:

We look for a small well-bred looking head and trunk, a clear confident eye devoid of piggish expression, fast easy paces, straight back and croup, wide loins and generally well developed bone and muscle... A very tall elephant is seldom a good working one... A smaller elephant than eight feet six inches will be undersized... A female makes the best hunting elephant, when she is really staunch with game, as her paces and temper are generally better... All elephants used for hunting must be very carefully trained and entered to their game. A good mahout, or driver, is very difficult to obtain. The elephant should first be accustomed to the firing of guns from his back...but their ultimate qualities will depend much on natural temperament. The more naturally courageous an elephant is the better chance of his remaining staunch after having been actually mauled by a tiger — an accident, of course, to be avoided as long as possible... It will occur sometimes...and then a naturally timid animal...will probably be spoilt for life, while a really plucky elephant is often rendered bolder...

Forsyth recorded:

In...April and May of 1862 I bagged six tigers and one panther in the Betul jungles, wounding two more tigers which escaped.... Another party was also shooting in the same district: and although they arrived after me in the field, contrary to the well-understood rule in such circumstances, proceeded ahead and disturbed the whole country by indiscriminate firing at deer and peafowl. It is scarcely necessary to say that when after tiger nothing else should be fired at. The Lalla (his favourite shikari)...securing a monopoly of information, in which he was well served by the conduct of our rivals in harassing the people in the matter of provisions and thrashing them all round if a tiger was not found for them... On one occasion I reached their ground just as their last camel was moving off to a new camp. They had stayed here a week trying in vain to extort help in finding a couple of tigers whose track they had seen. The tigers were all the time within half a mile of their tents; and before ten o'clock that day I had them both padded. During a whole month I believe they only succeeded in getting one tiger and that by potting it from a tree at night. Some years afterwards when I shot the same country under much more favourable circumstances, the numbers of tigers had greatly diminished, owing to the high rewards and the steady attention of the forest officers and my bag was then just the same as in 1862. Five or six tigers may in fact be considered a very fair bag

for one gun in a month's shooting, even in the best parts of the Central Provinces; but two or three guns, with a proportionate force of elephants, should of course do much better."

Forsyth went on:

Between five and six hundred human beings and an uncalculated number of cattle are killed by wild beasts in the Central Provinces each year... For some years heavy rewards were given for every tiger and other dangerous animal killed, special rewards being placed on the heads of man-eaters and I am convinced that many more were killed during that time than previously... The number destroyed increased every year... Rewards for the killing of 2414 tigers, panthers, bears and wolves were claimed in 1867 (the last year for which statistics are available) against 1863 in 1865. Tigers are certainly not so numerous by a great deal in many parts with which I am personally acquainted as they were even six or eight years ago...

Mentioning obvious changes which had taken place Forsyth stated that:

Jubbulpur is now rather an important place being the point of junction of the two lines of railway which between them connect...Calcutta and Bombay... At the time of which I write it was a small military and civil station... The steam horse has torn his way through the parks and levelled the bamboo clumps that were the glory of the place...

In *The Field* of 17 May 1862 Forsyth distinguished between panthers and leopards, pointing out:

the larger size of the panther, which reaches in fine specimens to seven feet eleven inches from nose to the tip of the tail, the leopard not exceeding five feet six inches; the lighter colour, and taller more slender figure of the panther and the rounder more bull-dog head of the leopard...

In writing about the panther he expressed unqualified admiration:

In my early sporting days I fell into the mistake of most sportsmen in supposing that the panther might be hunted on foot with less caution than the tiger. On two or three occasions I nearly paid dearly for the error; and I now believe the panther is really by far a more dangerous animal to attack than the tiger. He is, in the first place, far more courageous...if once brought to close quarters he will rarely fail to charge with the utmost ferocity, fighting to the very last. He is also much more active than the tiger, making immense springs clear off the ground, which the tiger seldom does. He can conceal himself in the most wonderful way...into an inconceivably small space. Further...he is far more difficult to hit in a vital place. He can climb trees which the tiger cannot do... And lastly his powers of offence are scarcely inferior to those of the tiger himself; and are amply sufficient to be the death of any man he gets hold of. When stationed...near Jubbulpur...I shot seven panthers and leopards in less than a month...chiefly by driving them out with beaters... One of the smaller species, really not more than five feet long I believe, charged me three times up a bank to the very muzzle of my rifle (of which I luckily had a couple) falling back each time to the shot, but not dreaming of trying to escape, and dying at last at my feet... When a panther takes to man-eating he is a far more terrible scourge than a tiger. In 1858 a man-eating panther devastated the northern part of the Seoni district killing (incredible as it may seem) nearly a hundred persons before he was shot... My own experience is that the majority of panthers that one finds are come across more by luck than good management.

Biased in favour of his Indian hunting as he undoubtedly was Forsyth admitted:

Few men would probably come to India merely to shoot over this central wilderness. But as a field for general travel and even as a sporting ground India is rapidly coming into favour among the wandering section of Englishmen...I will here speak only of the glorious field that country offers to the sportsman — incomparably the finest in the whole world. Africa may be thought to be better, but it is not so if India be looked at as a whole. Perhaps more animals in number or size may be slaughtered in Central Africa; but that does not surely imply superior *sport*. In reading accounts of African shooting I have often wondered how men could continue to wade through the sickening details of daily massacre of half-tame animals offering themselves to the rifle on its vast open plains. In India fewer animals will perhaps be bagged; all will have to be worked for, and some perhaps fought for. The sport will be far superior; and the sportsman will return from India with a collection of trophies which Africa cannot match. Africa and India both have their elephants. We cannot offer a hippopotamus; but we have a rhinoceros superior in sporting point of view to his African relative. We have a wild buffalo as savage and with far superior horns to the Cape species, and we have *four* other species of wild bovines besides, to which there is nothing comparable in Africa. In felines, besides a lion, panther and hunting-leopard, almost identical with those of Africa, we have the tiger, and one, if not two other species of leopard. Our black antelope are unsurpassed by any of the many antelopes of Africa; and besides him we have fourteen species of antelopes and wild goats and sheep in our hills and plains, affording the finest stalking in the world, to compare with the other antelopes of Africa. Africa has no deer, properly speaking, at all... India on the other hand has nine species of antlered deer. We have three bears. Africa has none at all. There is no country in the world that can show such a list of large game as we can in India. And for minor sport what can compare with our endless array of pheasants, partridges and wildfowl?

All this too is now so easy of access. Twenty-one days by overland passage lands the traveller in Bombay... If he joins a regular camp in the 'plains' he will find the most perfect system of open air life that has anywhere been devised...[with] pretty nearly everything that civilised man can want, ready to move about with him at the rate of from twelve to twenty miles a day. By the help of the railways he may see almost the whole country south of the

Himalayas and shoot specimens of all its game during the pleasant cold months from October to March...[or] combine with some small game shooting and pig sticking if he likes in November and December... By the time that April ushers in the hot blasts of summer he may find himself, if he pleases, stalking the ibex among the snows of Kashmir...

For mere sport England need not be left earlier than December... The help of the local civil authorities is of course of the greatest value; and I may say that it is always freely rendered to gentlemen projecting a tour through their charges. Some previous acquaintance with the language, and the general requirements of such a trip on the part of at least one of the party is almost essential to ensure success... The cost of such an expedition need not be very great. Most of the outfit required could be re-sold at the conclusion at no very great loss. One hill tent, ten feet square...would be sufficient for two sportsmen and would cost...about £30. A strong rough pony is the best animal to ride...(and) can generally be bought in Bombay at a cost of about £20... Arrangements should be made to get the loan of, or purchase, a staunch shooting-elephant and howdah...and a really good one will not be bought for less than £200 or £300. Decent shikaris can generally be obtained on the spot... The current expenses, after the outfit has been bought will come to about £30 per mensem of each sportsman...

It was obvious where his own sympathies lay, as he went on to explain how:

a man accustomed to rough it could get on and obtain the best of sport at much less expense than this, which is laid down for a party wishing to enjoy all the comforts of the Indian style of travelling in camp. Such an adventurous sportsman need only get for himself a small pal tent and a few necessary implements of travel and hire a camel to carry them, buy a rough pony for £5 or £10, hire a couple of servants and plunge with his rifle into the wilderness. If capable of speaking the Hindi language and conciliatory towards the wild men, he would soon have about him a knot of real jungle hunters who would take him up to every sort of game. Saddlery, hunting implements of all sorts...ammunition and clothes should be brought from England...

By 1870 Forsyth was writing, that following the 'universal introduction of breech-loading' he recommended a .450 or .500 Express rifle with short conical bullet:

for *all ordinary* purposes. For dangerous game such as tigers there is nothing better yet available for sportsmen than the large rifle firing the spherical ball, or explosive shell of my own invention, which I have described... All rifles should, by preference, be double-barrelled. To use a single barrel is to sacrifice many chances, while it possesses no advantage over a well-made double. A good price, however, will have to be paid for a really true-shooting double-rifle; and when this is a consideration a breech-loading single Express rifle will be found to give a wonderful command of shots.

He ended his outstanding book on Central India by recommending his gunsmith friend, Mr Henry of Edinburgh's, rifle as the best he knew. Towards the end of 1870 he returned home with his book ready for publication. Sadly in 1871 as the sheets were passing through the press, at the age of only thirty-three, he finally succumbed to the rigours of the life he had led. His book was thus published posthumously in November 1871, but remains an enduring record of the man himself and the sport he enjoyed.

With the 1870s the Edwardian era might almost be said to have dawned. It was the period of record game bags, when weekend shooting parties extended from Thursday evening to Tuesday morning, when parties went up to shooting lodges in the Highlands for the Twelfth and the deer stalking, when shooting big game in Africa or a tiger in India was the equivalent of the Grand Tour of Europe a century earlier. Driven game was the only possible sort of shooting recognized by most sportsman. There were first-rate sportsmen amongst both the men and women who hunted and shot, but hunting and shooting had become rigidly bound by class barriers which it was hard to surmount.

Driven game shooting was soon reduced to a science. Grouse and partridge driving were both sports requiring considerable skill, unless the birds were young, or had been driven until tired on the wing. It was thus that many bags of grouse were made early in August when many of the coveys were scarcely grown enough to fly, let alone be shot. Similarly partridges in September, although technically in season were often scarcely well enough grown to provide any sport. When either had been driven across the guns more than once in a day their speed was noticeably diminished and shooting them was that much simpler.

Driven pheasant shooting required woods laid out in suitable plantations, correctly placed to provide the guns with the most sporting and challenging shooting. The principle was to present the driven birds so that they were given the maximum chance and the waiting guns were provided with the trickiest shooting possible. Thus small copses on knolls would be driven out to guns sited in a valley below. In a flat country such as East Anglia this was not always possible and in some pheasant *battues* there it was not uncommon for overfed pheasants literally to be lifted up into the air by the beaters at the end of the drive, to flap their way over the guns and solemnly be added to the mounting pile beside each sportsman. Large bags in such circumstances were regarded by any true sporting shot with nothing but contempt.

In 1876 at the famous Norfolk shooting estate of Elveden, the Maharaja of Lahore, Prince Duleep Singh, deliberately set about the business of making record bags. He shot no less than 789 partridges in 1000 shots in one day and went on to shoot 2350 partridges in nine days. His friend Lord Walsingham, however, left him in the shade on 30 August 1888 on Blubberhouse Moor when he shot 1070 grouse to his own gun. Shooting with four guns and two loaders he crammed twenty drives into the day. It cannot be denied that it was a remarkable feat of endurance, let alone marksmanship. No doubt he had a gun headache the following day.

Prince Duleep Singh, Lord Walsingham, Lord Ripon and the extremely appropriately named Lord Huntingfield were amongst the select coterie of outstanding shots who were also close friends of Edward, Prince of Wales. At Balmoral in Scotland and Sandringham in East Anglia they helped to swell the royal bag at many weekend shooting parties.

Having started life as a gamekeeper in the 1840s, Thomas Speedy went on to become, with the development of sport as a tourist industry during the ensuing years in the Highlands and Lowlands of Scotland, one of the leading sporting agents in Edinburgh in the 1880s and 90s. He also wrote *Sport in the Highlands and Lowlands of Scotland*, from which the following on shooting grouse over dogs is extracted. Despite the somewhat archaic English the sport remains much the same today:

When grouse are plentiful on moors which are carefully burned, and where streams and springlets abound, they may be found anywhere and at any time. It is, however, where birds are scarce, and the ground not so favourable, that a knowledge of the habits of the grouse proves of much advantage to the sportsman. Should an early start be made, the birds will be found on the feeding ground — that is on heather of two or three years' growth. They generally repair to such places in the early morning to feed on the young and tender shoots; and if heather which is more rank be in the neighbourhood they will run into it to conceal themselves on the first indication of danger, where they will remain until their whereabouts are discovered by the inquisitive nose of the pointer. As the day advances, particularly if the sun be hot, they betake themselves either to the banks of streams, or to ground interspersed with ferns, bog-myrtle, &c., where they are often found when splendid patches of heather have been hunted in vain. As the evening approaches they again repair to the feeding ground. After having fed, they generally about an hour before dusk, resort to their roosting ground for the night. Should the sportsman, from any one of the numerous causes which render his day's work sometimes unproductive, or from his reluctance to return home without a good bag, be desirous to continue the sport, we would remind him that now is his opportunity. Let him start with fresh resolve, and follow the coveys to their resting place, where, after being gorged with their evening meal, they will lie like stones, until flushed one by one at the nose of the dog. Unless he be a most indifferent shot, he will in such circumstances have no difficulty in securing a good bag.

We once heard a sportsman who had studied grouse-shooting say — 'If I really wanted a heavy bag, I would not give the last two hours of the day — that is from half-past six to half-past eight in August — for any other six hours of the day.' He, however, remarked, 'that the fatal work done during those two hours with a good dog, partook more of the character of slaughter than of real sport. Rather would I bag twelve brace of grouse in the month of September or October, with their fine feathery legs and beautiful plumage, than thirty brace shot under such circumstances.'

Should the day be wet, the difficulty in making a bag is much greater. The grouse instinctively get on high and dry ground or bare 'nobbies,' where they sit motionless, so that the rain runs off them, aided by the natural lubrication of the feathers; consequently they do not get so wet as if their feathers were subjected to contact with the wet cover. From their elevated position they can observe the approach of men and dogs at a distance, generally taking care to be off before the sportsman can get within range. When such is the case, or at any time when the birds are wild, if a good bag be desired, the ground should be hunted in a systematic manner. Care must be taken that the ground in all cases be hunted against the wind, and when the dog points, then keep him in advance, so that the birds may be driven forwards, when the probability is they will be fallen in with again. Even wild birds, when driven forwards two or three times, will often separate and sit to the dog, and be easily bagged. Here it is important to observe that care must be taken to hunt the beat invariably from the boundary inwards, unless where the moor is so extensive as to render this precaution unnecessary.

When birds are wild, many sportsmen nowadays use 'Dart's kite' and keep it flying over the part of the moor being hunted. When, as a rule, coveys of grouse take wing long before they can be got near, single birds or pairs will lie like stones under the 'hawk' and thus the sportsman gets within easy range. When flushed, however, they dash off at such a pace that it requires an expert shot to bag them.

Quietness during grouse-shooting should be rigidly maintained. We have often seen the moor cleared of birds for a range of several hundred yards by people continually calling or whistling to their dogs. This to a real sportsman is simply intolerable. Many argue that speaking or whistling does not frighten grouse as much as the report of a gun. This is a mistake, as we shall have occasion to demonstrate when dealing with grouse-shooting among corn-stooks in a subsequent chapter.

There are few conditions which the genuine grouse-shooter will more rightly insist upon being observed while on the moor, than that of silence. Let us accompany a shooting-party thoroughly up to their work, and contrast their quiet business-like demeanour with that of the noisy and demonstrative amateurs and we shall perceive at a glance how desirable it is that unnecessary hubbub or noise should be avoided.

Two gentlemen agree to shoot together, and after a hurried breakfast jump on their ponies, or into their trap. The moor is reached, keepers and dogs are awaiting them, guns are taken from their covers, cartridges from their panniers and all is ready for the start. The dogs are standing in their couples, trembling with nervous excitement and pulling with all their strength in their eagerness to be let off. Let 'Grouse' and 'Nell' go, and the gillie in prompt obedience uncouples them. They are for off at once, but the word 'Down' reminds them they must wait till they get the order to start. Hold up 'Grouse' and with a wave of the hand to the right he is off at a rapid pace. 'Nell' is signalled to the left and promptly starts accordingly. Being jealous of 'Grouse' finding birds before her, she turns quickly evidently afraid that he will have anticipated her in finding game. She sees him galloping still on the search, follows him for a second or two, and than as if determined to have first point, takes a sweep round for herself. They range on both sides, quartering the ground and crossing each other with remarkable precision. In turning 'Grouse' finds himself close upon game and drops in the heather as if shot. Hush! the old cock's head appears above the heather; he sees the danger, and means to be off. 'Nell' has turned, and is coming right down on them. She will not get wind of them, and seems almost certain to put them up, To cry 'toho' is in all likelihood to result in the birds taking the hint and making off. Fortunately, she catches sight of

'Grouse' crouching among the heather and in an instant is as motionless as a statue. The old cock, seeing the danger on both sides, squats down in the hope of being unperceived. The sportsmen walk up to the dog, one on each side, and by encouraging him forwards, he crawls on his belly for a few yards, when up starts the covey. The old cock, as is customary, has by this time got ten or twelve yards ahead of the brood, is the first to rise, and consequently the first to fall. The other three barrels are discharged in rapid succession, when it is found that the old hen and two young birds have also fallen before the well-directed fire. The guns are loaded, 'seek dead,' and the dogs are not slow in finding them. They are picked up and admired and taken charge of by the gillie. If the party choose to follow the flight of the remainder of the covey, they may also be bagged without much difficulty. It is in such circumstances that the advantage of singling out the old birds — more especially the old cock — at the first rise, is apparent, as the young birds become scattered, and will sit so close as to admit of their being put up at the very nose of the pointer. It is at this point that the keeper discovers for the first time the character of the sportsmen. If gentlemen who have been frequently on the moors, the first shot

will be directed against the old cock-bird by the gentleman on the right or left, as shall be determined by the rise and flight of the birds. Again the remaining shots will in like manner be directed against the outside birds, each gentleman taking care that there shall be no cross-firing, but that he shall confine his attention to the birds rising on his own side. If experienced sportsmen the birds will also be allowed to fly a reasonable distance before the gun is lifted to the shoulder, so that while shot dead, they shall not be unnecessarily injured. They walk on slowly, taking care that every available bit of ground is carefully hunted and that the dogs have sufficient time to quarter their ground. They are always ready and when birds rise unexpectedly, owing to bad scent, or other causes, they are not taken at a disadvantage and thus a brace or two are generally added to the bag. When a single bird rises to the dog, as already indicated, it belongs to the sportsman to whose side it flies. We have often, however, seen a single bird rise and fly straight away without being fired at, neither sportsman wishing to deprive his companion of a shot. This, we consider, is studying etiquette a little too much, and ought to be remedied with an agreement that doubtful birds should be shot at alternately. Care should be taken that the birds when shot are carried by the legs in the hands of the gillies for some time, so as to allow them to cool and that they may be packed neat and carefully into the panniers. This to some may not seem of any importance; but a sportsman only once requires to see the baskets emptied after a day's shooting, to notice the difference between birds carefully packed and those tossed in by a careless and inconsiderate gillie.

When the sun is at its height — generally about one o'clock — sportsmen usually sit down to lunch. A place is usually selected by the keeper in a hollow by some limpid mountain-stream, and where there is a cool spring bubbling up from its channelly bed or gurgling beneath its rocky bank. The relish with which sportsmen enjoy their lunch during the glorious month of August in such circumstances is known only to those who have been privileged to realise it. The time allotted for lunch is generally not less than an hour, and, as a rule, is occupied with an agreeable chat; while among smokers 'the weed' is sometimes profusely indulged in.

As the success and real enjoyment of the afternoon's sport are sometimes determined by the character of the lunch and the liquors partaken of, we shall have something to say on this subject in subsequent pages.

After an enjoyable rest — the duration of which may be extended should the heat of the day be oppressive — the party again fall into line and recommence their sport. For a little, unless fresh dogs are uncoupled, the pointers will appear stiff and rather lazily inclined; but if they have been brought into good condition before the season, they will, on finding game, be inspired with renewed energy. If fresh dogs are let loose after resting at mid-day, so much the better. Where this cannot be done, the dogs while resting, may be indulged with a sandwich or a piece of bread; as it is scarcely to be expected that a dog which is fed only each night — once in the twenty four hours — however willing, can stand out for eight or nine hours without nourishment.

It is in the afternoon when the sun is past the meridian, that the sportsman frequently finds exercise on the mountainside or around the base of some heather corrie most enjoyable. At the same time it is generally from two to four o'clock that complaints of the scarcity of birds are most frequently made. How often has the question been put by gentlemen who are not mere novices in grouse-shooting — How comes it that it so frequently happens that there are so few birds to be seen at this time of day? It is obvious that it is not because the birds are fewer in number upon the moor, but simply they are not to be found in the places where they are sought for. As previously explained, during sultry weather, and in the middle of the day, grouse, as an invariable rule, betake themselves from the high ground in large numbers to the banks of burns, or ground interspersed with ferns, bog-myrtle, &c. While good average sport may be relied upon, even by those not fully acquainted with the habits of grouse during the afternoon, it is, as already indicated, when evening approaches that they can be more easily fallen in with. The scent at this time becomes better, and as the birds are scattered about feeding, they are more readily picked up by the dogs. If on a beat near the lodge, sportsmen will frequently shoot homewards, and unless in view of some definite arrangements, will generally be guided by circumstances as to the hour of their return. If engaged on a beat several miles from home, however, arrangements will have to be made to meet at an appointed place at a given hour, where the trap and horses will be waiting to receive them. Punctuality in such cases ought ever to be studied so that everything like irritation and annoyance may be avoided, owing to any of the party being kept waiting — by no means an unusual occurrence. Attention to this simple rule will contribute in no small degree to the winding up of an agreeable day's shooting. At the close of such a day's sport as we have indicated, the trusty keeper will realise a sense of relief; while his duties, though arduous, will partake more of the nature of enjoyment than toil.

In 1889 Charles Lancaster was to write his book *The Art of Shooting* which deservedly went into thirteen editions by 1964 and remains good reading today. The splendid period pictures demonstrating shooting and gun safety are today perhaps as much an attraction as the instructions themselves. His chapter entitled 'Etiquette of Shooting' remains as sound today as when it was written:

A great difficulty here presents itself to the author, because this Treatise is not written with a view to telling the sportsman how shootings should be managed, game reared and found, or ground worked to obtain the best results. Many good works have been written on these subjects and to them my readers are referred. I will, however, just mention a few of the most important facts to

be remembered when shooting in the company of others.

Be careful to carry your gun in such a way that it never covers your left-hand gun. It is not pleasant to find the line being broken in walking, owing to the 'left' guns hanging back to escape looking down the muzzles of your barrels.

Etiquette in the field often prevents a word of caution being given to a careless man, although a retiring or shrinking away from the line of his gun may have the desired effect

In covert, just as much care should be taken, as the careless handling of a gun by one may spoil the enjoyment of the whole party.

For the same reason do not disturb game by laughing or talking loudly when walking in line, going to your stand, or waiting for the drive the commence. You will have earned your invitation if you can persuade the wags and chatterers in the party to be silent at the right times.

Always allow pheasants to rise sufficiently to prevent a dangerously low shot being taken. Although the effective range of a shotgun is about 40 yards, remember that individual pellets may fly 200 yards or more with sufficient force to wound.

Once one of a party managed to give me a good 'dusting' in the following circumstances; — A rabbit was seen in the covert we were facing, when suddenly it bolted out into the ride and came towards me in a direct line. I saw the next 'gun' about to shoot. I shouted, 'Don't shoot!' but too late; he had fired; the shot glanced from the stony ride and 'dusted' me all down one side.

This shot was made by a man who should have known better; and it so impressed itself on my mind that I cannot help mentioning it here, as a caution to others who might be tempted to fire such a shot. Many persons may probably have had a similar unpleasant experience.

Never fire at a bird too near; because, if a kill is made, the game is so dreadfully mangled as not to be worth picking up. And never shoot at too long a range, as the tendency is to wound; and a bird so struck is seldom recovered, but gets away to die a lingering death. Such shooting is unsportsmanlike and cruel.

Be careful never to shoot across your next gun, nor take his bird. If, however, you notice that you have 'divided' with the next gun an equidistant bird, it may be possible to avoid discomfort or controversy by tactfully delaying or hiding your reloading. If you fire slightly before your neighbour, remember you will hear both shots, but only one may be audible to him.

Cultivate the habit of looking cheerful, particularly at the end of each drive. This costs nothing, helps to induce the frame of mind in which you shoot well, conceals your disappointment if you have done badly, and shows your host, his keepers and beaters your appreciation of their hard work to provide you with sport.

Chauncey Hugh Stigand was an accident-prone big-game hunter with a very staccato style of writing. In his book *Hunting the Elephant in East Africa*, published in 1913, he wrote:

In 1905 I was looking for elephant in the vicinity of Fort Manning. I had no thought of rhino...I met a fresh spoor...and...bent down...to see the tracks...I heard the engine-like puffs of a pair of rhinos close at hand... The next moment a great behorned head burst out of the grass a yard or two from me. I had no time to think, but just shoved my Mannlicher in his face and pulled the trigger. He swerved, but...at the same moment I became aware of the second one bearing down on me from my left. There was no time to reload, so I tried to jump out of his path with the usual result in thick stuff that I tripped up.

He kicked me in passing, then...whipped round, and the next moment I felt myself soaring skywards. I must have gone some height as my men on the elephant track said they saw me over the grass which was ten or twelve feet high... I fell heavily on my shoulder blades... I looked round for my rifle and...picked it up...while doing this I suddenly found that a finger nail had been torn off and was bleeding. Directly I discovered it, it became very painful.

Whilst examining this injury some of my men appeared and uttered cries of horror. I could not make out why they were so concerned till I glanced at my chest and saw that my shirt had been ripped open and was covered with blood whilst there was a tremendous gash in the left side of my chest, just over the... heart...Small bits of mincemeat were also lying about my chest and shirt...

I felt nothing at all except a rather numb sensation. It struck me that it must have pierced my lungs; I would soon know if this was the case, as I would be spitting blood. I waited a short time and nothing of the sort occurred, so I concluded that the lungs were all right...

I was about thirty miles from Fort Manning, and...I started back to the nearest village. After walking (my horse) some time I felt faint (but) I...performed the rest of the journey on foot.

Having arrived at the village...I dressed the wound as best I could and lay down...I had a sleepless night until about two in the morning...

A friend then fortuitously appeared with an Indian doctor, who 'stitched the wound up most skilfully...three weeks later I was well enough, though still in bandages, to start a 240 mile march, which I completed in ten days.' Stigand was killed in a native ambush in 1919.

Of much the same vintage was James Sutherland, another Edwardian big-game hunter who died in 1930, still hunting big-game to the last. In his book *The Adventures of an Elephant Hunter*, published in 1912, he described his feelings on returning to Africa. He recorded:

The morning coat and silk hat I wore on my last brief visit to England I flung into the sea in sheer exuberance of spirits, when I left Marseille, glad to be quit of such costly insanity...

He wrote succinctly on wounded elephants:

...If I merely wound an elephant and he bolts I make every effort to follow him up and finish him and I am glad to say that in the majority of cases I accomplish this end. I adopt this procedure apart from the question of obtaining ivory, for in my hunting I have always endeavoured to bear in mind the question of pain. Swift death is comparatively little to any living thing — long drawn out pain is terrible, and when the question of hunting is concerned the professional is usually too experienced a shot to entail any unnecessary suffering on the animal he hunts...

Such men, of course, had total contempt for the large driven shoots and the Edwardian liking for record bags of game, current at this period. Yet with the slump in farming and farm values from the 1870s onwards, much agricultural land was worth more for the game shooting than to lease as agricultural land. The shooting rent and the money made from trapping rabbits was often the difference between survival and bankruptcy for many farmers during this period.

As already noted a sport which had really only begun to be at all well known in the second half of the nineteenth century was red deer stalking in the Highlands of Scotland. This has since remained popular only with a few because it is anyway limited by availability and also because it requires at times both dedicated enthusiasm and considerable physical fitness. A great deal, however, must of course depend on the ground and the circumstances. No two stalks are exactly alike. Therein lies much of the fascination of the sport.

In the Edwardian era some of the English owners of the shooting boxes which had sprouted like fungi all over the Highlands had reduced the physical exertion required when stalking to a minimum. The night before the stalk gillies would be sent to the tops of the neighbouring mountains with flags and instructions to raise a different coloured flag in the morning according to whether a good easily stalked head was visible from their vantage point or not. When the telephone had been developed wires were laid to each viewpoint so that the gillies could explain the conditions. The chief stalker would then lead the English laird, or his guest, up the hill on the back of a sure-footed hill pony to within easy stalk of the stag. He would then lead the way in the stalk itself to within as close a range as possible, before handing over the rifle already loaded.

When the stag had been shot, it would be gralloched (i.e. gutted without ceremony) and loaded on to the back of another pony, while the shooter would be solemnly congratulated. In due course the antlers, or the stuffed head, would grace the walls of his home as a trophy.

The alternative picture was one of very hard work indeed. If it was raining heavily, as it frequently was, the stalker soon found himself well soaked. A day spent in fruitless stalks in such weather conditions, up and down four-thousand-feet mountains and rocky faces or sliding scree, soon convinced many that stalking was not for them. Once shot, the stag had to be hauled to a position where it could be loaded onto the pony or into a boat. This could be left to the gillie or the work could be shared. The genuine sportsman always shared the heavy haul and on the top of a strenuous day of perhaps fifteen or twenty precipitous miles this could be a very testing trial indeed. There were few social pleasures involved in this sport.

Throughout the country at this time already it was noticeable that many years of intensive game preservation and 'vermin' killing had radically affected the wildlife of the countryside. Many once common birds and beasts had been so harried by gamekeepers and naturalist/collectors that they were now rare to the point of extinction. The osprey, for example, was no longer to be seen and the marten was almost extinct. A society for the preservation of fauna was formed as early as 1903, but initially had very little effect on public opinion. Only a few far-sighted sportsmen and naturalists saw the need for some form of action to rectify this one-sided state of affairs.

The rigidity of mind of the period is perhaps typified by the fact that at this time the spaniel supporters were having a great deal of difficulty in obtaining the recognition of their dog's all-round abilities in the field. Gundogs had already been classified as pointers and setters or retrievers. It required much impassioned argument before the spaniel was eventually accepted as a third category of 'utility gundog'.

By this time repeating shotguns were being produced and great numbers of cheap Belgian shotguns were flooding the market. The rabbit, after years of encouragement, had reached near plague proportions in many areas and was the centre of a thriving industry. Shooting in East Anglia or on the moors still attained high standards. The Great War of 1914 brought it all to an end.

The Boer War between 1899 and 1902 had affected the whole country in a way no war really had before. Yet the sporting tenor of the countryside had remained much as usual. Familiar faces might be missing, sometimes for ever, sometimes to reappear bronzed by tropic suns, but hunting and shooting remained virtually unaffected. In the First World War of 1914–18 everything ground to a standstill. Huntsman and gamekeeper, master and man, joined the forces as the magnitude of the struggle began to be appreciated. Hounds were put down and only skeleton breeding packs retained. Hunt horses were requisitioned for cavalry. For the first time women appeared as Masters of Foxhounds, carrying on while the war lasted. Shooting ceased to be a sport and became again a means of obtaining food. Game preserving ceased and poaching flourished unchecked.

With the end of the war came the inevitable aftermath. Recovery was slow and painful. Heavy taxation and inflationary rises in the cost of living made the old spacious Edwardian way of life an impossibility for most people. In the early 1920s agriculture, which had boomed during the war, was once more sacrificed to the townsman's cry for 'cheap' food and again Britain's farmers found themselves 'farming rabbits' in order to survive.

As far as shooting was concerned, most of the old estates had been forced to let their shoots to syndicates of friends or businessmen, who shared the expense of the upkeep. Such syndicates had been known, but frowned upon, in Edwardian days. Now, as a practical means of maintaining the sport, they proved a reasonable compromise between giving up altogether, or continuing as nearly as possible in the old manner. Admittedly there were usually less gamekeepers than in the spacious days, and possibly less birds were reared, but this may have been no bad thing.

Sir Peter Mackie's classic *The Keeper's Book,* (first published in 1913) still makes interesting reading and in the foreword to the seventeenth edition, published in 1929 he wrote with considerable foresight:

In a quarter of a century there has been progress not only in methods and the technical development of sport, but in its economic importance and to a certain extent in the opposition to it. The growth of the English industrial town populations and the journals which cater to this class have accentuated the difference of outlook which exists between the town-dweller and the country-man. An extremist group of misguided and unduly imaginative folk are

definitely against all 'blood sports,' i.e. shooting, hunting and fishing. Their avowed object is the legal prohibition of all sport. They are blind to any side of the case but their own, and they do not at the moment represent a serious menace. On the other hand, it would be idle to suggest that all the measures on our Statute Books have been placed there because they represented the genuine opinion of the majority of voters. Political experience suggests that any organised minority with funds may succeed in pressing through legislation which affects an unorganised majority. The majority of voters are uninterested in any question which so far as they can see does not affect them personally, and in any intensive political campaign fact and truth are apt to be lost sight of in a mist of distortion and propaganda.

The economic side of shooting is far more important than the average townsman knows. He does not realise that sporting rights are proportionately as valuable to the farmer freeholder as the greatest estate owner. Still less does he realise that except for the amenities of sport, the countryside would lose many of its residents. The local shopkeeper may not realise to what extent the claims of sport affect many of his best customers. It is not a matter which one can definitely balance in the account books, but in general it is a matter which should be borne in mind by all concerned — and mentioned whenever casual conversation swings round to anti-sport talk.

It would be difficult to assess the amount of general unemployment caused if shooting were to be prohibited. It is not only a matter of a catastrophic fall in land values and, so as many parts of Scotland are concerned, ruin to landowners and keepers alike, but it affects gunmakers and...skilled craftsmen. Millions of cartridges are fired in a year... We can wipe out the gamefood industry, we can take a substantial load of traffic and passengers off the railways, reduce motoring a little, hit the sale of tweeds and generally carry the ever-widening ripple of our devastation farther and farther afield.

Viewed in this light we can count the probable costs of sentimentality — ?, but it is also fair to question whether any direct benefit would occur to the animal world in general by the relaxation of our present system of preserving. The experience of the war years (1914–18) was that lack of keepering meant an entirely disproportionate increase of vermin — who did not confine their attention to game, but made matters worse for the farmer. Nature is a good deal more cruel than man, but the sentimentalist seldom knows anything about Nature at first hand...

After his succinct Introduction it is interesting to find him writing on the pheasant as follows:

Prior to the war the rearing of pheasants had been overdone. It had become artificial. In many cases a larger number of birds were reared than the land would carry. Complaints by farmers and agitation started by cranks, against all forms of rearing and game-preserving were the result. It is to be hoped that in the future this over-rearing will cease, and that sportsmen will be content with smaller bags of wild pheasants, and only rear a supply sufficient to maintain a good stock — shooting few hens, and after the first shoot, only cocks, and these only high birds...

After a period as a schoolmaster at Stowe, in the 1920s and early'30s, T.H.White decided to stake his future on making a living as a writer, as chancy an occupation then as now. He was to make his name eventually with his delightful series on the young King Arthur *The Sword in the Stone* and *The Witch in the Wood.* He also wrote *The Goshawk,* a classic account of his attempts to train a young hawk. The extracts presented here are from his lesser known book, *England Have my Bones,* to write which he spent a year living in a country pub in Northamptonshire, fishing, shooting, hunting and learning to fly, while keeping a diary of events. A descriptive and honest writer, if not always the best or most experienced of sportsmen, his account of shooting in 1934 read:

September 1934

I was invited to shoot at Gallowglass, walking. There were eight guns, and I was at the end of the line between Peter and Charles. We started at 10, but I didn't get a shot till about 11.30. Then Harry, Colonel Southcote, an unknown, and myself lined a hedge, with John on the other side of a narrow spinney at the bottom of it. The rest walked two fields towards us. They sent over a covey of about 40 at Harry's end of the line. I am not sure whether he fired, but at any rate he did not get one. They swung down the hedge. The colonel browned them, missing with both barrels. This spread them. Anonymous missed with both barrels. The air was full of them, like a handful of brown clods. I picked the birds and startled myself out of my wits by getting a left and right.

It was the first shot at partridges on the first day of the season. The hand shook which evicted the cartridges and I couldn't help doing an embryo war-dance, walking in two quick circles. A little after, a covey of seven got up in a stubble field, by the keeper on my left. They swung across. I had my first barrel killed, and my second hard hit. Peter missed. Then nothing till lunch. Then nothing till 4.30, except that I missed two rabbits — confused by dogs, cows and too many guns. But I had better face it and admit that I could never kill a rabbit. At 4.30 we met the big covey again, right at my feet. I killed two with my first barrel, one with my second. The rest of the day we walked roots, up and draw-back empty. I had a chance at two birds. The first was a silly miss in a long cross-shot. I shot behind him. The second was slain between myself and the twins. I don't like walking close as it is difficult to decide whose bird it is, and I get flurried.

Finally I ended by failing to kill a very high pigeon and at that moment two partridges came over the hedge, with the wind, to find me with an empty gun.

We had 23 brace of partridges, about six of rabbits and a brace of hares. Harry had four brace. Peter had a brace and a hare, plus rabbits.

It was a lovely day, bright with hundreds of small well-shaped September clouds, and a thunderstorm in the evening.

Shooting is a pleasure which depends largely on the moods of the country. It comes too at a time of the year when men begin to feel a call upon their resources. There is a nip in the air and one can detect the winter coming. So it is a call to endurance, a bracing challenge which makes life far more virile than the supposed provocation of the townsman's spring. In the winter people are in general much more convivial, much more strenuously red-blooded, than they are while the sun vitiates them. And yet the sun is pleasant. In September, over the cracking stubbles, the two seasons meet....

11 September 1934

We shot over Williams; one of the nicest days. I heard rumours of what was to be expected, from Bourne after accepting. I was afraid that they were going to shoot pheasants (which they were) and lodged a strong, tactful protest at the first opportunity. To Williams' immortal credit, he thereafter discouraged it. What a circus! Any keen policeman would have run us in at sight. One man was completely round, a sort of perambulating carbuncle, and one had a vermilion nose, and one looked like Pistol. The first thing Williams did was to clean his gun, with a pull-through, that hadn't been cleaned since he shot last year. Then we set out, about 3 o'clock.

The place was thick with birds. I think we saw 200. Everybody was in command, everybody pointed his gun at me, nobody did more than put his safety catch on, even if he was climbing through a blackthorn, and the wings were generally about 20 yards behind the centre. The keenness was high. One charged off in any direction that took one's fancy. Williams, the excitable Welsh angel, never saw a covey but what he wanted to follow it wherever it was going at once. There were the sheep dogs that charged about in all directions whenever a gun was fired off. At one stage two people had been left (abandoned without notice after being placed for a drive, which was dropped at the last moment) half a mile behind; three more, myself included, were lying on our backs in a valley; and Williams, with other ebullient spirits, was crawling about a bed of bulrushes, some hundreds of yards ahead. I was furiously angry, resigned, delighted, by turns, and shot like an idiot, but that didn't matter.

We had nine brace (including one young pheasant by mistake) and a few rabbits. There were seven guns. I had a brace and a half to hand, one shared, and a wounded brace never picked. There was never time to pick anything. I missed the easiest shots I had, but it was a splendid day. One high, just shootable partridge went down the line unscathed, drawing ten cartridges. My only decent shot was a close bird that had to be taken close, or else somebody else would have had him or me, whose head I almost blew off.

I remember hitting a bird which looked as if it had blown up (the feathers) but was never picked; walking a large field of stubble with my right-hand neighbour's gun pointing at the pit of my stomach; deciding never to invite Secker (who shot the pheasant) over my own land, but breaking that resolve; refraining with difficulty from shooting Williams, who suddenly drove his car down the edge of a full field of roots, shouting in a stentorian voice 'Where are they?'; missing the easiest shot of my life, and the most difficult and two of the oddest; the fact that practically none of the party could button up their waistcoats on the right buttons; a really masterly drive (organised by me — in temporary though divided command) being ruined by the other wing (which wouldn't stop) and forcing me to fire at a covey of about 40 (which would, if the other wing had stopped, have swung right down the line) when crouching half-way through a barbed-wire fence with a barb in my behind (the bird turned and was not picked) and Williams' amazingly hospitable high-tea afterwards, everybody lovely and hungry and only one tie between the lot of us. I don't know when I enjoyed a day more, taking it bye and large. Jimmy Warm shot his first partridge, with tremendous secret joy, just breaking silence. There was an early morning mist and all was piping hot. Tomorrow is the first day over half my own little rough territory. I shall have to say my prayers tonight.

Brown retrieved her first bird. She has been a trouble and is going to be.

12 September 1934

I woke up with a pain in the top of my belly — some form of indigestion, I suppose — and had to rush about with the final arrangements of telephoning and luncheon, before I went up early to Wood Fields.

The place is of 500 acres (37 woodland, and I should think a good 50 arable) The shooting shared between me and Mr Bourne. I pay next to nothing, and we split the game and rabbits, and Tom has the reasonable option of shooting when I do.

Harry Southcote and Jimmy Warm arrived at 10.20 a.m and we pushed off with four guns. We killed a rabbit and a brace of partridges skirting the N.E boundary, myself on the boundary wing, well forward. Luke Fieldfare (late as usual) found us when we were on the Close boundary. We swung round the plough stubble and reached the roots without seeing anything.

The roots showed some birds — say 50 — I got a brace on the right wing.

Fieldfare's brother-in-law, Aytoun, turned up at about noon, and somewhere about that time Tom Bourne went off to Camford. This left us four guns, counting Jimmy. We had three dogs, a blind labrador belonging to Aytoun, Fieldfare's spaniel, and Brown. With this contingent, now that we knew what was what, we set out to do the business. At about 1.30 we decided to give the Wood Field's roots a rest (we had combined walk and drive about 3 times across them) and paid a flying visit to the other territory.

This consists of the farms of Wilson (150 acres at the Old Inn, half — almost — arable) Tilly at Chackford (250 acres) and Robins towards Park (70 acres).

We just took the stubble and roots of these, once through, and fetched a brace off each, with one over. I had a tremendous high shot in Wilson's on the left wing, a miracle.

We had a dust up before going back to Bournes. So much necessary humility in learning to fly has made me autocratic on the rebound; and in any case autocracy is essential in the shooting field. It is the same as an army; and shooting, like all joys, is a serious business. It was a grand day at Williams', because I did not have to feel responsible for making a show of birds. As a guest one can afford to be irresponsible. As a host it becomes an altogether different business because the sport depends up on oneself. And if it is going to be good sport, it has got to be controlled. However unimportant the shoot may be, it is worth running it with discipline, so as to kill more birds. In this way the legendary colonel, with a high blood pressure who has a fit if a gun gets a foot out of line, is worth having as a host. Anyway, I came back, right or wrong, with a chastened line. It was over an illicit rest for beer; and I am now faintly ashamed of having made a fuss.

In Wood Fields we didn't do much more. The day ended, to all intents and purposes, with four birds down between Harry Southcote, Luke Fieldfare and myself — of which I felt inclined to claim left and right, one shared.

We ended with 11½ brace, a brace of pigeons, a hare and some rabbits. I am satisfied with this; for it was practically speaking to four guns. Harry Southcote shot beautifully getting 4½ brace

Aytoun shot with a 28 bore. He is the best shot that I meet among the farmers, although he is not a farmer and not local. An ideal shooting companion, he relishes walking on the wings and kills scientifically and never counts or claims his birds, and is always in a sunny humour and doesn't spoil his quite remarkable dog. It would be nice to have a world of one's own and pick this kind of person to live in it.

Harry Southcote was walked off his vaunted feet when we stopped, and had to beg for mercy

Brown hunted a runner, quartering exquisitely, and picked it up, and more or less brought it to hand. I climbed a fence and patted and cheered her; which, I believe, was wrong.

The birds were wild, the cover inadequate and there was no close shooting.

I put up 5 hen pheasants.

I think on the whole the host gets most fun out of a shooting party. Although the worries are trebled for him, the corresponding delights of strategy and tactics amply make up for them. Just as it is a real tragedy to see a covey go sideways out of a drive, so it is a real delight to see one's plans work out. If there were ever sensitive and intelligent generals during the war, I believe they must have sampled the depths but also the peaks of human achievement. One is being a general, on the humaner scale; pitting one's wits against the animal kingdom; balancing wind, weather, season, habit and experience against one another. Also it is pleasant as Sancho Panza remarked, to have command — even over a flock of sheep. It is exciting to ask opinion, but not to tolerate it unless asked, and to match it up in one's own mind and to accept responsibility.

17 September 1934

We shot over a farm at Southam belonging to the Derbys. They are giving it up on the 29th and want everything killed before then.

The 29th is New Michaelmas Day, the date on which farm leases expire. It is one of the regular dates of the country year in the Shire, like the 15th of May for shooting rooks or the Easter Bank Holiday for planting potatoes in the allotments. You don't get a rook pie often nowadays, yet it is very nice. The birds are skinned, not plucked, and only the legs and breasts are used, along with all sorts of tasty additions like onions and eggs.

We started at 1.30, Luke Fieldfare, Frank Derby, John Brown, Watson, a clergyman and myself. The clergyman was a magnificent surprise, a voice so fruity and ecclesiastical that he continuously seemed to be imitating himself. He was not in a clerical collar and we did not catch his name. On being introduced to Luke, a churchwarden, he said 'Ay think ay've already maide your acquaintance at the archi-diaconal visitaytions.' Luke said: 'What?' The cleric said;'At the archi-diaconal visitaytions.' Luke said; 'Where the hell's that?' To which the clergyman replied: 'Yew wouldn't say that to the Bis-hop.' This was a good start.

First of all the shooting was rather a circus, only the clergyman was worse. We careered about and the birds were as wild as we were, so we never got up to anything before the church had sent it away. He generally popped up in front of a line of walking guns and said: 'All the birds have flown away. Ay can't think whay.' In the end we lined for a drive. I got a left and right but one was a runner who was not picked through running down a rabbit hole in view.

Then it began to pour. It rained as if it would never stop, and Luke was in the middle of a vast field trying to pick up a wounded bird and the rest of us stood under a hedge talking about ecclesiastical matters. After hours of this John Brown and Watson decided to pack up. I think we only had 1½ brace.

Luke and Frank Derby wanted to stop, but were not convinced. The clergyman, who was evidently a very valuable person, wanted to go on — we were far too wet for it to make any difference — and I lay low, determined to put off the parting as late as possible. Brown and Watson definitely went. Luke tried to, but we kept him in the car drinking beer. After half an hour it looked as if it might just clear, so we waited.

To be rewarded by a brilliant evening, with 7 brace of partridges, 4 hares and 13 rabbits. Of these I killed 2 brace, a hare, 4 rabbits and walked the wing all day in prodigious manoeuvres.

Luke got his first left and right that I have seen today. Frank Derby was mad on hares and would suddenly break the line and dart away with his gun at the high port, and chase them for miles. I was pleased with my hare, stone dead in a flabby somersault and a cloud of moisture, and my rabbits. Ground game improves

18 September 1934

I suddenly had a bye day over my own territory at about two hour's notice. We started at 3 in the afternoon, after I had spent the whole morning trying to get Williams, Derby, Secker, Brown, Watson, or anybody else to come. But it was market day; and there was some sort of sale in the neighbourhood in the afternoon so they all refused. At any rate they can't say I haven't asked them back, and it has been a good thing in a way. We started at 3, an amazing collection of marksmen. There was Major Ninton and his son walking, Jimmy Warm, Tom O'Connel, Allweather (the sergeant) and myself. At about 5 o'clock Mr Bourne joined up over his land. Birds were scarce and wild in the east. But we ought to have had 3 brace there. Nobody hit one at all, though the major just hit me, from the opposite end of a very long line.

At Bourne's the marksmanship improved slightly but the generalship declined. I left Bourne to do our second and third drives, driving to self and Ninton and Jimmy, and somebody spoilt them — thereafter blaming Tom O'Connel. The latter must have had a sad day. He was slightly browbeaten by me, for not shooting at birds at 25 yards; he missed everything; he was rated by Tom for spoiling the drive, which as a matter of fact had been equally spoilt by all the walkers; and he ended by spraining his ankle. I gave him a hare and Ninton took him home.

But to get back to Bourne's. We put a good 40–60 out of the roots, and the sergeant got 2 by browning and Tom missed, and Jimmy was too shy to fire. I killed a hare. The drive through the famous holding grass field then took place under mismanagement, and yielded a solitary frenchman, who came over about 20 yards to my left and I killed him by luck. Then I went to turn them at the hedge between two poor fields, whilst the guns swung inefficiently round a third. Here everybody blazed away at hares, and the sergeant killed one. We then went round again and I spoiled the manoeuvre myself, by not going right round the plough, and lost the birds to our right. I had also missed both barrels in the east, total bag: 2 brace; 2 hares, 1 rabbit. It ought to have been seven brace (to ten if Tom Bourne's drive had come off). My main recollections are of people not firing when they might have done, and of blaspheming audibly.

But I have paid off my invitations, and learnt a lot. You don't enjoy the smooth without the rough, and this shoot is certainly that.

The sergeant is good to watch. Ready — Present — FIRE! He looks as if he was bayoneting Germans.

26 September 1934

We had half a day over Derby's. The church was again represented and behaved as usual — a grand person. There were also Frank Derby, John Brown, Watson, Luke Fieldfare, self and five beaters. We got 4½ brace, 3 hares, 11 rabbit. Of these I had 1½ brace and an odd one picked up running ten minutes after a drive, which I suspect was mine from its position. But I am sick of shooting jealous. It is one of the things which don't seem worth wrangling about. It is worth being proud of what one does, but only when it does not admit of question, as in fishing. Good resolution from this day forth; never to claim a bird, even if there is no doubt at all. It would be nice not even to keep a count of one's birds, but I don't think I can rise to this obviously proper attitude yet.

The wind was amazing. I should think it was a gale nearly; at any rate the wireless had a gale warning last night, and the birds came over like bullets, streaming with the wind. Everybody was missing like hell, including Luke. Although I managed to get two of the driven birds, one of them a single straggler, I was shooting ill. I missed two easy shots, also a rabbit. Proh dolor! Old John Brown, the ground game shooter who leaves the birds severely alone and shoots with number fours, wreaks great havoc among the rabbits. He canters along in rather an aimless way, and today wiped Watson's eye most beautifully — killing a hare that I should have left alone (and I seem to take things up to 70 yards) with one barrel after Watson had missed quite close with two. Watson had shot at a sitting hare scandalously, and missed it, so I was delighted.

But what a wind! You could scarcely tell they were partridges before they were gone.

It poured at the end, a thin driving shower, and my twa-snouter bonnet was worth its weight in salmon. Luke said to me 'You'll be able to circumvent them to-day, they won't know whether you're coming or going.' I said: 'Yes, and if only I was a clergyman I could wear my collar back to front as well.' But the church didn't mind. He shot a rabbit eventually.

29 September 1934

We had half a day over Luke Fieldfare's, driving, killing 16 brace and 3 hares or it may have been 5. This was an instructive day, when it comes to shooting jealousy. I had a brace and there were nine guns so that I must have been slightly above the average. But how can one have an average at shooting? The first drive and the second did not give me a shot. I was on the wing. In the third I was in the middle and this was easily the best of the day. The birds came over quicker than one could load. Fred Aytoun on my right was missing finely. After four minutes we had time to breathe and count — a brace each picked, and heaven knows how many poor creatures may have gone away to tower a couple of fields off or with dropped leg. There was no time to look behind. This was the best four minutes this season. The one drive yielded 6 brace to the line. Then there was a drive that showed me nothing on the wing. Then I shot a single bird that swung down the line walking and thereby wiped an anonymous eye. Then a single bird was presented to me on the wing and I shot it. Then two more drives showed me nothing. So five drives came to me without a shot. Supposing I had been lucky in my place (and Luke did not place us, but left us to scramble, and I was too much the dirty gentleman to thrust into the middle) I might have had four brace instead of two. Supposing on the other hand that I had not been in the middle for the third drive, I should only have had a brace. It seems to me impossible to compare a bag with the next man's when everything is such a matter of luck. The only sense in counting one's own heads is so that one can add them up at the end of the season...

1st October 1934

The first of October. I got up at 6.15 and went to the home field to see if any pheasants were peeping out of Roof House. The sun was due to rise at 6.45 or something preposterous like that (it is fine to feel condescending towards the sun himself, in respect of early rising) but it was quite light. There were no pheasants. I tried all my outlying coverts — The Renford Cabbages, etc — but nothing. Back for breakfast at nine and had a fine bath, reading the morning paper as I was not working till eleven. Then I earned my living until

101

12.45 and fixed up the riding after luncheon; fed my pheasants; took an intelligent beater to explain the drives at Three Woods; and went by appointment to the Ransomes to slay a cock pheasant who was alleged to inhabit an abandoned kitchen garden. We walked all through the nettles, thistles, grass and dock without putting him up. There were Bill Ransome, Ker, Mrs R. with an untrained cocker and myself. We were all wandering rather aimlessly when two hen pheasants that had been sitting tight (with recollections of Williams next door I suppose) got up in front of Ker — who missed.

They came across me, a beautiful chance for a left and right, but I only hit the front one hard. She threw up her head and went on, scattering feathers, into Williams' osiers. I did not expect to see her again, but got over the wall with a vague idea of searching. Just then, whilst I was changing my cartridges, somebody put up the cock, who came straight over my head — a magnificent sight, wings spread, tail streaming high up. By the time I had got some cartridges in, he was at the nadir. I covered him wildly and pulled, but the safety catch had stayed on in the flurry. So he waits for another day. In a little while Bill brought the cocker to seek dead in the thick osiers. To my astonishment, as well as to everyone else's, she walked straight onto the first hen, stone dead; a magnificent piece of work.

Then I worked again until 5.45 when I tried the verges of Roof House in a rain storm, and finally back to dinner and to work till 10. Tomorrow the cock and today there is a hen's tail feather in the twa-snouter, on the first day of the pheasant season.

9 October 1934

This has been a queer week. On the 5th I had a day over my own with nine guns. The first and best drive of the morning was wrecked by Luke Fieldfare, whom I had left to direct the walkers whilst I placed the guns. He had arrived $^3/_4$ of an hour late to begin with; bless him.

Unfortunately I introduced him to Mrs Ransome before giving him his instructions and this went to his head so that he did not listen,

'Do you hear, Luke? I want them driven towards the house.'

'Yes, old boy. Yes Mrs Ransome. Sit down, Timmie!'

'You know; the way we did it before.'

'Yes Mrs Ransome. Yes old boy. Timmie, sit!'

'You do understand, don't you?'

'Sit down, will you. Yes. Yes, Mrs Ransome, of course.'

The result was that he drove the roots parallel to the guns instead of towards them. All the birds went across us, and I was as rude as I could be to him, in front of everybody. More strained relations.

The next thing was that as soon as we had reached a critical field, with forty or fifty out-manoeuvred birds before us, we would find a decrepit old labourer in the middle of it, gathering mushrooms, and not a bird to be seen. This happened twice. From Wilson's, Tilly's, Brown's and Higgins' we only got a brace.

Then a difficult lunch. Then, in my best drive of the day at Bourne's, Luke, Fred and another breasted a ridge above the kale, arm in arm and talking loudly, whilst they were taking position for the drive. The two main coveys of 18 and 21 left at once. I had warned them of this before, and fairly lost my temper — offering command to Luke and refusing to take any more responsibility myself. There was nothing left for this drive except a couple of coveys at the beaters' end and these they succeeded in letting out. So it went on. We could get nothing out of the wood — though this was expected — and the day ended with about two brace, three hares and a few rabbits and pigeons.

I went out next day with a boy to help walk, and shot a brace in Wilson's — left and right — I also missed a hare.

On the 8th I went out again with a boy and missed a cock pheasant with both barrels.

On the 9th I went out again with a boy, and killed a brace at Bourne's — left and right. I missed a rabbit and hit a hare in the quarters with No 6 shot at a long range. Any decent person would give up shooting so far....

11 October 1934

Today Tom Bourne rang up at 2 o'clock and said he was going out for rabbits round the hedgerows with a friend; would I care to come? I went till 4 o'clock. We had 3 rabbits, 1 leveret and 2 partridges. I was on my day, for of these I had all but one rabbit. There was a possibility that I had another bird which towered but was not picked. They are going to look for it this evening. If found this will make my third consecutive left and right on partridges, which is not bad for a feeble shot, under varied conditions.

13 October 1934

Luke Fieldfare's. We had seven guns and slew five brace, four hares. I had a brace and a hare. They were high swinging birds, everybody missing. Made it up with Luke, who was as nice as could be. It was a happy day.

The pleasures of shooting in the Shire really depend upon the unimportance of the sport. In evading all extremes we have evaded being a shooting county. A few, very few, great houses preserve their game; but apart from that we are not fanatical. There is little to be satisfied with and so we have to be satisfied with little. This is pleasant

The sportsman is happy out of doors even without his gun, or without using it. One day last spring I was walking round Three Woods to keep down the young rabbits. I came out of the wood stealthily and there were two pairs of pheasants. The further pair saw me first, because they were outside the long grass and made for safety in the characteristic pheasant way. That is to say, the hen flew and the cock ran. Cocks are cowardly. I suppose because nature does not have to manufacture the male to withstand pain as she does the female. Then the nearer pair saw me, and the hen flew at once; but the cock squatted.

His head shot up vertically out of the grass when he noticed me and vanished instantly with the same sort of motion. I thought; 'Very well, you crafty old devil, I shall give you a fright.' I began to walk up towards him, anticipating with pleasure the terrific leap of agitation with which he would leave the ground if I could get upon close. But suddenly, before I had come within thirty yards of him, there were a hare's ears in front of me in the long grass. She seemed to be feeding quite unconsciously, and the big furry cavities, like ship's ventilators, turned this way and that. I went slowly to within a couple of yards without disturbing her, but the moment I stopped she was off. Her ears went flat, she puffed out her body as if she were taking a great quavering breath, she nerved herself to the effort and then she was bounding away. Her hind legs lifted her behind. They are longer than the forelegs, and this, I believe, makes hares run faster uphill. I put up the pheasant afterwards, but somehow he was not important after puss. She faced me dead on, as she was taking her breath, and so I could see the two eyes set square back in the sides of the head; eyes which seem not to see very well forwards, so that hares sometimes blunder into you if you are directly in front. I had approached her from dead ahead, and perhaps this is why I got so close. I have remembered her for six months and now write her down, thinking of the bright salmon pink blood on the hare's cleft nostrils that I harled and slung over the hasp of a gate at Luke Fieldfare's, six months later.

5 November 1934
Guy Fawkes Day. Up at 6 o'clock and got to the lake for an indeterminate dawn. The three tufted (if it was the same three..) were on the octagon, on my side. I had been trying to get a duck for Laddie so long, and was so enraged at the two losses of last week that my morale gave way, and I sent them the choke barrel on the water. For one thing, it was the only way of making them get up and go over Laddie. But it was blood-lust that did it; quite, pure, unreasoning, unsporting. Blake would have approved. It knocked two of them silly. I went for the punt. The third went over Laddie and vanished. When I was just coming out of the boat-house one of my two came to its senses and flew away, a tough specimen. I picked the dead bird.

Till eight o'clock I made manoeuvres round the Oxford water and Copper Bottom trying to drive things to Laddie.

On our way there we found the spare tufted on the Eleven Acre. I put Lizzie on the high dive and gave it the cylinder at 80 yards from the reeds on the other side to move it. It went over him beautifully and he missed both barrels.

I killed a sitting rabbit, or practically sitting. He just unsat.

Immediately after breakfast we went up to the home field. Tommy Roberts shot his pheasants at Roof House on Saturday so there were hopes. They were fulfilled. We saw four hen pheasants and a cock running into the bracken as we arrived. I hurried round to the Roof House fence and left Laddie to walk them up, assuming that he might get the first shot and I the second as they came for

Roof House, if he missed. But we could put nothing up. One hen broke at last, well away to my left. I fired the choke first, and must have missed, for she looked in range. I then gave her a hopeless cylinder out of temper. She went on her way rejoicing.

We kept at it, beating bushes and wandering about. At last I spotted the cock, making a dash from a bush and ran like a lunatic to put him back. Succeeded. I sent Laddie to the bush and he put him out rather clumsily missing both barrels

In the afternoon we made a round tour, partly thwarted by rain, labourers in stubble fields, and Wetherby's beagles. So that we couldn't get up to anything; except a silly hare, who came loping towards me end on, at half a mile an hour, and was duly slain.

I also missed a snipe with No 4 shot and felt perfectly certain I had killed him dead; a characteristic of snipe, I suppose.

6 November 1934.

Up at 5.45 and down to the lake in the night darkness but we did not get a shot... Then to the borders of Roof House and slew yesterday's hen pheasant. She seemed Mongolian or Chinese. Saw no others...*The low-down on sitting shots:* My duck, rabbit and hare yesterday not only gave me no pleasure, but also made me feel miserable for them. I felt that I had murdered a live thing. To-day's pheasant, who was crossed off neatly, first barrel, on the wing, did not inspire any feelings of pity at all. It was not a live thing murdered, but a good shot. One is a concrete assassination of beauty, the other is a creation of beauty — the beautiful aim.

Shooting sitting is not unsporting, but unsatisfactory. It produces no elation and so leaves time for remorse to breed. No art has compensated the destruction which one is left to contemplate. A mere dead hare; horrible. But a hare cut over so that he somersaults with his head on the ground; beauty.

8 November 1934

I should like the people who kill bags of a thousand birds to have been with me today and I wonder whether they would have enjoyed it. I was up at 5.45 and met Laddie between the lakes. It was a grand frosty morning, and as soon as the sun came, he came in red, tinting the thick hoar saffron, between the melted patches where the sheep had been lying down. It had been a duck's frost. The octagon was frozen, the Eleven Acre half. I sent Laddie with my gun, round the Eleven Acre in a wide circuit, with instructions to stand at the gap nearest the Boating island. I took his four-ten. After giving him a full eight minutes and now it was light, I walked down the north bank, where I knew they would be. They were and I sent two flights of about eight each exactly over the gap. He, however, had posted himself by the bathing shed. Not a shot...

We went up by the tennis courts and a rabbit ran into a bush. I shot into the bush, two feet in front of me, as he went in and broke a back leg. You always seem to break the back legs of rabbits. This was my only barrel. Laddie, instead of shooting him as he crawled across the path, dithered and ran. He got away, to die horribly, I suppose.

By the tennis courts a cock pheasant announced his invincibility, quite close. I ran round his plantation, to the Doric Bridge, leaving Laddie to come through from the temple. But there he was, crouching like a domestic hen that wants to be mounted. His shoulders were high, his neck and tail well on the ground. I was torn between emotions. On the one hand a pheasant is a rarity to us, and a good thing to show off; on the other hand, I get no pleasure from a sitting shot. But I had only the four-ten. Could I risk waiting till he flew? I aimed at him like the most determined murderer, and fired. He got up with a tremendous start, leaving six body feathers (two cut in half) and flew straight to Laddie, not rising very much. Laddie missed him, and he vanished in the trees where Laddie forgot to mark him down. So I have the satisfaction of knowing that 1. I have shot a sitting cock. 2. He is lying dead somewhere, without being any good to anybody. It is like murdering an old lady and then finding that she has pawned her jewels. We searched for twenty minutes and gave it up. Among other things I know now that it will be lunacy to start next season without a good dog, however expensive.

The home field was blank and I got back for breakfast at 8.

I worked till 12.30 and then went out again, with 3 sandwiches, Robin and two boys. It rained continuously till sunset. I missed one rabbit. Robin shot a weasel (locally called a wizzle). My efforts to drive a few coveys over him were frustrated by each of the boys in turn; one by shouting a loud question at the wrong moment; and the other by waving his arms. I walked the whole afternoon trying to send things to Robin, in vain. The birds are now more cunning than carrion crows. At about 3.30 we thought it might be worthwhile to beat a bit of the wood. Unfortunately Robin started off in the wrong direction, lost himself, and remained lost for nearly an hour. In one way this seems very funny, but it frightened me at the time. I had heard his gun go off when he shot at a pheasant and thought he must have killed himself. At dusk we got back to the car; and ate sausage rolls, bananas and cheese sandwiches (with coffee) by the light of the roof lamp. It had been a completely blank day and we were soaked to the skin. I stayed in my bath (with Sloan's Liniment in it) for an hour and a half reading *Dos Passos*.

9 November 1934

Up at 5.45. But yesterday's red sun was right and the afternoon's drizzle was still going on. It was muggy. Saddened by experience of Laddie, I decided to put myself in the proper gap and leave Ker and Robin to turn them to me if they could. At least I should get a shot as they came in. Of course they didn't come.

It seems a boring thing to record the time of getting up on a blank day. But shooting of this sort, like fishing, is not boring even when it is blank. It is not only lovely to get up when everyone else is asleep; it is lovely merely to stand still while the sun rises, to have one's gun weighing on one's arm, and, with the faculties all alert to be *patient*, absorbed in a place and attitude...

The very first of January 1935

I got up before 7. There were no duck on the lake, and the snipe was absent from the Camford water, Bourne's rushy wild, by the cabbages, was blank. Jimmy and I went up to Three Woods and split to go singly round the sides, meeting at the top. I saw a pheasant go in almost at once, and went to the place in which I thought it had settled, without any particular hopes. The wood is hopelessly thick. However, this or another pheasant got up at long range, and I just had time to change my finger to the choke barrel. She was a hen, and I turned her over beautifully into the thickest of the undergrowth. I spent an hour trying to find her, tracing lines from the first big puff of feathers, to a further couple in a thorny inferno, but in vain. At 10 we came away after I had lost my temper. At 10.5 we met a hare in a hedge and were both too surprised to fire. At 10.7 Jimmy shot a rabbit; and I missed in a brambly ditch what may have been a rabbit or might have been the hare. It is not even certain I missed it. Everything was too dark, impenetrable and hellish to be properly sure. Anyway, I gave it up. At 10.30 were driving back when we spotted a cock pheasant scooting across the road into my land. We stopped the car and surrounded him. However, he saw us both and got up almost out of range. I gave him both barrels hysterically, and he seemed to throw up his head a little for the first. He came down in the next spinney, beyond the Camford water. I ran to circumvent him, stalked the spinney inch by inch, spotted him crouching under a root as cunning as a tom cat. The usual internal struggle, then I retreated half a dozen paces and gave him the cylinder barrel sitting. He jumped a few inches and lay still, bleeding from the beak, a beautiful bundle of mahogany, an old spurred cock. I went back to Jimmy and lied that he was a broken-legged bird that I had to finish off as a runner.

After breakfast I went back to borrow Bourne's Pip, to search for the first bird. Scent was hopeless. Pip got into something and lost herself. This wood is a genuine *selva oscura*. One scratches oneself all over, staggers, almost cries, tussles like a Laocoon. At last I found the dog and started back in a Livingstone-Stanley detour, to a place where I *thought* I had last seen a hen come in. On the way, with boughs between my legs and brambles round my neck, I thought I saw a woodcock, but had no chance to fire. It was a brownish silent blur that banked. It may have been an owl. Pip worked beautifully. In the patch where I had expected the pheasant, there she was. But I was far off. She got up quietly and there was a tree between us. I changed to the choke, thought she was out of range, waited for the tree, and turned her over. Both this shot and the first gave me a shock, but I daresay that a closely-packed wood of trees makes distances seem larger. In this case also Pip failed to find; but luckily I walked into her stone dead, a dark coloured bird. I am invited to Milton on Saturday.

5 January 1935

It was the Milton Saturday, with twelve guns, the last pheasant day of the season. We had something over a hundred birds between us. Two-thirds of the guns were lame and the rest asthmatic, but it was a revelation to see them shoot. All the birds collected in their last corners, and then began getting up like a *feu de joie*. I don't know whether it was having been ill, or a desire to excel and consequent poking, or sheer incompetence, but I only got four birds all day, and this made me miserable. The birds were surprisingly silent, coming from distances, and they curled over beautifully, head under, tail over, as the other guns shot them. I remember one bird, hard hit, wriggling in the air above me in the effort to go on, like a Chinese dragon. The grey long-tailed flakes floated out of the high woods, to be curled up in delayed puffs before you heard the bang.

I don't know what I was doing wrong. I was probably poking and pulling to the right, and the birds directly over me seemed to be a bother. It was a humiliation; but as I always do it at a big shoot I had better get accustomed to the feeling. I don't get enough shots at pheasants...

Milton is one of the great houses that preserves. There seem to be no points of comparison between this great kind of shooting and my own, but it is lovely to have a little of it now and then. It is lovely, for one thing, to see a troop of

keepers again; their weathered hands and faces, their tough boots, their rainproof clothes, their sure movements. Keepers seem to look after their masters like nurses. It always amuses me to see a man carrying a gun or some cartridges for another grown man who is going to use them. Then there is the luxury of a shooting luncheon, with an appetite for the tasty food and the sloe gin, and a roaring fire in a barn or parlour to eat it by, and jolly company, and out again to the suffocating excitement of the big drives and the flakes floating over from far and leaping up from near, so quick, in the last minute, that you have to let the birds go by.

7 January 1935

Milton again, with the same guns nearly. A general, a colonel and a captain, all excellent shots; another captain and the host, moderate; a youth, name unknown, and a one-legged gentleman named Weakly; Also 2 keepers carrying guns. This made 8 official shooters, plus 2 unofficially. We were doing a last general clean-up and got 32 pheasants, 23 brace of partridges, nine hares and a couple of rabbits... Today I killed 3 brace of partridges, 3 hares. As usual I missed every pheasant of the four that came to me. I suppose I shall have to get psycho-analysed. Of the partridges I had one left and right, single birds, ten yards apart.

I enjoyed myself. It was an odd thing, but I suddenly found myself limping in sympathy with the rest.

Damn the pheasants.

Alas!

Just lack of experience at this grand kind of shooting, I suppose.

19 January 1935

Martin came with Tom Bourne, Jimmy Warm and myself. We went up at 6.30 to the lakes for duck; to Three Woods at 10.30 for the wood; back again to walk the hedges with Pip at 2.30. Meals at home. We had 1 cock pheasant, 1 hen mallard, a woodcock, 1 hare, 2 rabbits. I was lucky and shot all but the pheasant and one of the rabbits. There are six woodcock in Three Woods. 2 snipe in the bog, 1 snipe at Camford water. These must be seen to.

Totting up my records for this season, I find that we have killed 97 head of all sorts on my tiny rough shoot so far, of which I have killed 49. In shoots to which I have been invited we have killed 363 head of which I have killed 49.

I can't help feeling that today's bag has its own kind of fascination. No doubt I should have a tremendous shoot if I were a millionaire and I daresay I should get bored with it. But here, where you have to rise with the sun and walk all day, and earn what you kill, and be satisfied with little or nothing, it does become a kind of achievement to make one's own little gamut. We only killed seven things, but they included five separate species, and we saw six. Each shot was a separate affair, widely spaced from the last in point of time, and earned by the exercise of one's own legs. This *workmanlike* type shooting trains one to a special kind of shot. One doesn't become a *good* shot, like the automatic butcher at the *battue*; in fact, one remains, in comparison with his type, a very poor shot indeed, but I think one keeps a kind of emotional advantage. It must become boring to be a great shot, who stands while the keepers deliver. For one thing it must become easy. And when easy it ceases to be satisfactory, like all other achievements.

15 January 1935

Martin shot one pheasant and self one rabbit. There were eight pheasants roosting in one tree, but this is the time of year when the pheasant's novelty begins to lose its flush. It is the woodcock and the snipe that steal the lustre. I was far too pleased yesterday after killing 2 'cock, to be able to trust myself in writing about it. But the fact is that I am a good shot at 'cock, probably because as an emotional shooter it suits me to fire quickly without giving law. I seem to kill them before they have begun to slip, as snipe and woodcock do.

They are both difficult birds to shoot and where I was brought up there used to be a rumour of a half-crown sweep in every 'cock. The lucky man received half-a-crown from each of the other guns. I tried to persuade them yesterday to give me some money, but they wouldn't.

31 January 1935

At Milton to finish the partridges. Eight guns killed 16 brace, of which I killed 3 brace; of 9 hares I had one. This is now the third time this season that I have been invited to the great house, and I am very lucky for an ordinary Shire-man. If you look at it on average, it is few of the average men who get the chance of a big shoot, even if it is the end of the season. We have to tip, of course, and as every keeper can tell you it is the poor man who gives the biggest tip, generally with the best grace. We don't want to let ourselves be overawed. But it is worth the tip. When we have worked the whole season for fifty brace, it is grand to kill fifty brace in a late-season day. It is lovely to have everything working perfectly; and to draw for places out of a little silver cylinder; and to move up two automatically; and to have our choice of whisky, beer, sloe gin and cherry brandy; and to feel a warm sort of affection for the host who treats you so well; and there is always the shooting, too, the plethora of birds that it would take ourselves a week to see, and the fact that at *partridges* we can shoot as well as the big guns.

Michael Bratby and Peter Scott were friends as young men in the 1930s with several somewhat specialized interests in common: painting and punt-gunning, geese and wildfowling. They shared a punt and met together whenever their work allowed it at a lighthouse on the Wash. The following extract is from Michael Bratby's book *Grey Goose* and is entitled 'Punting at Brents':

Colonel Peter Hawker used to shoot swans and he considered them the kings of wildfowl, abandoning everything for the chance of a shot at them. But if he

thought of swans as kings, then geese were princes, and the only geese he knew well were brents. In his time great packs of brents visited the south-coast harbours, and in spite of the constant stream of aggravations with which, according to his memoirs, he was forced to put up, he managed to shoot a great many in his lifetime. Nowadays few wildfowlers shoot swans, but geese remain as the principal prize, and even if there are not so many as there were in the Colonel's day there are still a few places left which provide flocks which would have delighted his eyes. Every punter must have experienced the feelings which prompted the Colonel to rail against the constant misfortunes which seemed to dog his path — the scarcity of wildfowl, the unfavourable weather (though perhaps we don't get quite such extremes these days), the wildness of the birds and the pop of the shore-shooter's twelve-bore just as the punt is drawing into range. (I suspect that our modern shore-shooters would not be pleased at being referred to in print as 'that unrivalled garrison of tit-shooters'.) Over one hundred years ago the Colonel, in a fit of bitterness after an unsuccessful day, wrote 'It is all up with gunning.' Although at that time he was undoubtedly taking a gloomy view, and this was proved by the many splendid days he was able to enjoy subsequently, it would be very much more appropriate now, for his own favourite harbours are no longer suitable places for wildfowl and little gunning is done in them. Possibly the south coast has suffered more than other parts of the country, but the chance of stalking brent geese is nowhere so easily come by as not to be regarded as something out of the ordinary.

Every year, a flock of brents come to the Wash. They do not arrive until after Christmas, and the size of the flock varies. The north German coast — winter haunt of thousands of brents — is barely three hundred miles away, and if the weather there becomes hard it is not a great distance for a goose to travel, so that the number feeding on the little Zostera that remains on the Wash often changes considerably during the last two months of the season.

During the last week of February — and of course of the shooting season — Peter rang me up from the Wash to tell me that some five hundred brents were 'in' and to suggest that I came down with the punt. We had several times

stalked very small lots of brent on the Wash, but never a flock anything like as large as this one, so I was keen to go. It was not, however, until the week-end, that I was able to get down to the lighthouse. I arrived on the evening of the twenty-eighth of February to find the wind blowing hard and cold from the north. We sat round the roaring fire, hoping that the morrow would bring slightly more inviting conditions for punting. Strong winds help punt gunners in some ways and hinder them in others. Birds sit closer together when it is blowing hard and they are also less inclined to fly, but on the other hand it is difficult to push a punt as it should be pushed with the wind ahead or abeam, and short choppy seas, such as are set up on the shallow channels of the Wash, soon make a punt a very uncomfortable and wet place. It is so low the smallest seas break inboard and the floor becomes a very disagreeable place on which to lie.

When dawn broke the following morning the wind, far from moderating, had increased, and wisps of snow whirled round the lighthouse. The fire burned brightly inside and the punt remained, forlorn and lonely, on its trailer. There was plenty to talk about and it seemed silly to go out. Still it was the last day of the season and there *were* five hundred brents... Just before lunchtime we decided that we ought to do something instead of spending the whole day gossiping. We put on a great number of sweaters and went outside. It would have been idle to pretend that the prospects were inviting, but we decided to take the punt round to the creek which was nearest to the mudflats on which the brents had last been seen, and to launch her there if we felt it was worth while... Our creek was several miles to the north of the lighthouse, so we arranged to meet towards evening so that the motor-boat could tow us home.

As we stood in the mud at the edge of the creek in which we were thinking of launching we heard the brents calling outside. The die was definitely cast and in a few moments the punt was sliding and slithering its way into the creek. So comparatively close were the brents that we had to keep down from the start, although to begin with the walls of the narrow twisting creek gave us a certain amount of cover. Through the glasses we could see that the brents were swimming in shallow water, eagerly awaiting the appearance of the banks on which their lunch grew. The tide was ebbing fast and before we left the cover of the salting the geese were standing on the wet mud and our chances of getting to them had vanished.

I held the punt against the side of the creek where the last few tufts of grass grew on either side of it. From our prone positions it was impossible to see whether our creek would lead us anywhere near the geese or not. All that was visible was acres and acres of mud, with the edge of the ebbing tide some half a mile away. The geese, by this time completely clear of the water, were feeding greedily, though from time to time small parties flew round, giving us a faint glimmer of hope that one of these flights might top the edge of our creek.

We pushed on down the creek, hoping to find that it would bring us nearer to the brents. The pushing was very difficult as for most of the time we were driven by the wind on to the lee-shore, where wave after wave of cold, muddy water clopped into the punt, so that it soon covered the floor-boards and gradually seeped through our clothes. When things looked at their blackest and thoughts were turning from geese to lunch, a remarkable change in the situation suddenly occurred. Our creek joined a larger one and, as we entered it, the beam wind came astern. The bed of the larger creek was hard and sandy, whereas the old one had been muddy, holding the setting-pole like a glue-pot and making each stroke extremely difficult. Most important of all, however, a large proportion of the brents, suddenly flew off the high mud and settled on the banks of the very creek in which we were, only a few hundred yards below us. With the pushing straight forward and easy, and the wind to help us, we made splendid progress. As we drew near, however, we could see that all was not going to be plain sailing. Between the punt and the main lot of geese was a small bunch of about fifty birds. They were sitting on a small spit of mud which ran out into the creek. It was most unlikely that these geese would allow us to pass them, and if they rose the chances were that they would take the big lot with them. It seemed a pity to shoot at the little lot, with such a chance within our grasp, so I asked Peter what he wished to do. 'The near lot aren't worth anything. Try to pass them,' he whispered. To do this I had to swing the punt out into the channel to avoid grounding on the shallow which is always found near a point such as the one on which the thirty geese were sitting. In the middle of this operation Peter said: 'We'll never pass them. Take them.' When he spoke the punt was almost broadside on to the geese although we were early in shot. As I struggled frantically to force the bows round so that the gun could again bear on the geese, I saw out of the corner of my eye that their heads were up and I knew that in a second they would be off. Aided by a few desperate stabs the bows swung round, but just before the gun could bear we grounded on the shallow, and we were stuck. Another second and the geese were up. As they crossed the muzzle Peter fired. The smoke cleared and I could see that we were lucky. It is impossible for anyone who has not pushed a punt to realise the relief that comes when the smoke clears to reveal a good shot. It is a wonderful feeling of a hard job well done and of relief at being able to stretch cramped muscles. We had been lying down in the punt for nearly two hours.

When the shot was fired the work was by no means over. We had a tremendous chase after two winged birds which took us right out into the open waters of the Wash, for, swept away by the ebb, they could swim almost as fast as we could row. When we returned to the scene of the shot the dead birds were lying right away from the channel, the tide having ebbed fast. As we gathered them up the sun broke through and a patch of blue sky appeared. The wind had not abated, nor had it become any warmer, and there was a black cloud on the horizon which seemed to promise more snow or sleet.

We baled out the punt which had become very full during the stalk, and looked ruefully at the horrid muddy, wet mess which had been our lunch. It reminded me that we were hungry and, somehow, that we were cold, and for the first time that home was a long way off. There was no time to talk so we stowed the birds, congratulating ourselves on the best shot we had ever made at geese of any kind, hoisted the sail and set off. The heavy cloud brought with it sharp squalls of wind and sleet, and the darkness began to close in. At first we made good progress, the punt scudding over the water at a great pace, but presently the wind came too much ahead of to sail with advantage, for a keelless punt makes much leeway. Rowing was difficult in the short seas, but the tide had turned and it now helped us. From time to time we eased on the oars while Peter tried to pierce the gloom with his glasses in the hope of seeing the motor-boat. Many times our hopes were raised, but the distant mast always turned out to be a beacon or some piece of wreckage.

As the last signs of daylight faded away we gave up hope of rescue and resigned ourselves to rowing the six or seven miles which still separated us from home. If all went well we should be in by ten o'clock, but we should have a fair wind for the last part of the journey, and that would enable us to sail once again. Still, it was not an inviting prospect and in the dark anything might happen.

We had started to row mechanically, only talking at intervals, when suddenly there was a light ahead. It was Johnny, swinging a torch in the bows of *Havelle*. It was a tremendous relief. In a few moments we were aboard, making the painter of the punt fast to the stern of the motor-boat, In the tiny cabin the stove glowed and a kettle sang cheerfully, and as we sat round telling our story and hearing of the adventures of the others it would have been impossible to imagine a cheerier party.

Several incidents occurred on the way home. The engine stopped ('It's full of water,' said Johnny), we went aground ('We'll have to be careful of her,' said Johnny. 'She's so rotten, you could spit through her if you had a mouthful of peas.') and the punt which we were towing overturned, probably because we were going too fast in the rough water. This last was the most serious misadventure, but luckily we had taken everything of value out of the punt, and by dint of manoeuvering in shallow water we eventually righted her. It was nearly ten o'clock when we reached the lighthouse, to find the cheerful fire still burning and the even more cheerful smell of dinner awaiting us. It had been a splendid day and one we should always remember, but the worst was to come. I had to be at work in Manchester at nine o'clock next morning, and as I went up to bed I thought... 'Manchester is 170 miles away. That means getting up at three, or at half-past at the latest if we're to have any breakfast and I am *tired*.'

When the alarm clock went off, well...

Supporters of *battue* pheasant shooting, the really large shoots, with bags of several hundred head of reared birds, have always been hard to find. There is, undeniably, something distasteful about shooting birds which have been reared, however successfully, like poultry, simply to be driven over the guns at the end. Unless the birds are well presented and challenging shots, the reared birds well mixed with wild birds, they are only too often simply not worth shooting and the *battue* lives up to its heavily criticized reputation. There are, of course, exceptions, but sadly few.

It is noticeable that Sir Peter Mackie warned under the heading 'Pheasant' in his knowledgeable work on gamekeeping: *The Keepers' Book* '...whether feeding the hens in...covert, or the young broods at a later period, there must be no attempt to call the birds by whistling to them when about to distribute the food. This bad habit tends to domesticate the birds to a marked degree...' Later on he added another point on feeding often overlooked: '...Too much maize should not be used; it makes the birds heavy, yellow-fleshed, and not agreeable to eat... Overfeeding and waste are generally rampant in places where pheasants are reared. Most birds get 40 per cent more food than is necessary...'

It is, perhaps, a little unfair to include William Bromley-Davenport's advocacy of *battue* shooting at this stage, since it was originally written by this Victorian writer in the 1880s. There was then a good deal of ill-informed criticism of this form of shooting in the cheaper tabloids. The article was, however, printed again, in the 1930s in a book with a foreword by Lord Newton entitled simply *Sport*. Even though *battue* shooting was in its heyday when he wrote, Bromley-Davenport clearly found it somewhat difficult to describe it interestingly, as the events of such a day, while exciting to those taking part, tend to have a certain repetitive monotony when described in print. He wrote:

...we will imagine a scientifically-organised and faultless shoot...with six good guns and coverts full of game, a kindly and courteous host, a fine morning in the latter half of November, a slight frost having now (10 a.m.) given way to a bright sun and gentle south-westerly breeze. We proceed to the first covert, a small clump in the park... Hazel slips stuck in the ground about eighty or a hundred yards from the covert, with a small piece of paper in a cleft at the top, mark the several positions of the four forward guns, whom the host now numbers off to occupy, taking the *others* with himself to walk in line with the beaters. For a time not a sound save the gentle tapping of the beaters, sticks is heard; there is no shouting, no 'Hi Cock!' or wild yelling, which is deemed so indispensable at uncultivated *battues*... Then a shot or two, followed by several more from the inside guns, who are now warmly engaged with the rabbits, then the first pheasant — an old cock — is seen by the forward guns sailing silently along just over the tree tops towards them. His outspread wings do not move, he had attained his requisite elevation and impetus when he rose before the beaters to clear the trees at the further end of the clump. He is lowering now, and apparently thinking of a descent to earth just outside the covert, but catching sight of the guns forward he re-agitates his wings and ascends again, as though not fancying a too close proximity to these four suspicious little groups of beings. These groups (of three persons each, i.e. the shooter, loader and cartridge carrier) on their part are watching him anxiously. Whom will he come to?...number two fires, and catching him at exactly the right angle he collapses...and his body falls with a heavy thud just behind... Knocking down your game and killing it are two very different matters. There should be no flustering, or spinning in the air, or easily inclined descents, followed by, Oh, horror! active pedestrianism on the ground. Too many feathers left in the air indicate too great a proximity to his tail; they should be few and small, struck from the head, neck and breast only. So should the 'rocketer' fall; as straight to earth as the velocity of his previous flight, or the force of the wind will allow, and, falling, never move so much as a feather...

Then follow a few more birds equally distributed among the four professionals and disposed of with equal science. Then a few hares come cantering out midway between the guns, offering fair broadside shots, and are rolled over stone dead by well-laid forward-aimed guns; no piteous screams or erect heads, as they drag their broken hind legs after them, no coursing by retrievers, as would occur when a 'muff' is 'behind the gun'. They turn head over heels and never move again. And now the pheasants come quicker and the firing becomes fast and furious, till behind each gun lie many little feathered lumps of varied hues on the smooth turf. Now and then, though very rarely, in the hurry and heat of the action, even these professors shoot a little behind a bird, and he carries on sorely wounded, but is usually marked down and gathered by watchful keepers, who stand with retrievers far behind the guns. Sometimes, too, though still more rarely, the very best professor among them, with an almost world-wide reputation will 'clean miss' an easy shot. And now many of the pheasants will no longer face the forward guns and curl back over the beaters' heads only to meet their doom from the two guns who are now standing back in the covert. As the beaters close in a semi-circle at the end of the clump, the laggard birds only rise just at the fence, and give lower, nearer and less interesting chances. These seem the easiest shots of all, but they are not so;...perhaps because the shooter has to look all round him to see that no stray keeper or retriever is in the way before he fires...

...The host and his companion emerge...hopes his friends have had good sport, pays a well-placed compliment or two to those whom he has especially observed... The keepers and beaters collect the slain, and they all hurry on to the next covert. Fear not, reader! I will not repeat the dose... Enough to say that, as was inevitable with fine weather, plenty of game, good management, and first-class guns, the head keeper at the end of the day, with a face radiant with satisfaction, hands a card to the host, who enumerates large totals to his gratified guests. The result is that the keeper is pleased; his birds, so long carefully tended, have been 'clean killed'...the host is pleased, for the totals are even more than he expected, and if these amounted to even four figures, what harm? Who is injured by it? Not the tenant farmers, many of whom are out beating, or looking on with smiling faces...taking as much pride and interest as the host himself in the successful proceedings, and who, with half the neighbourhood round, receive handsome presents of game, and what else can it hurt but the proprietor's own pocket? For these *battues* are costly. Still, if he likes to spend his money thus, employing as he does a great number of persons, what harm?...'

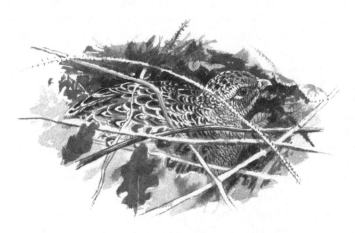

'The Boxing Day Shoot' by Julian Tennyson from his book *Rough Shooting* published by A & C Black in 1938 is a classic of its kind. Julian Tennyson was killed in the war, but his book remains in many ways a very evocative record of a day's rough shooting. Although describing a small and friendly day's driven shooting on a rough shoot (i.e. without a keeper) before the war, the day could in most respects be taking place today. Many driven shooting days on keepered shoots, both then and now, could fare worse and vary very little in practice. The narrative has the unusual advantage of explaining why various drives are chosen, which is always a matter of concern in any day's driving and should always be subject to change if necessary owing to alterations of wind, weather, or other unforeseen happenings, even on occasions in the very largest organized driven shoots when things have gone awry. It also gives the beater's and pickers-up's viewpoints, which are not always clear, or sometimes, sadly, of great interest to many present day game shots.

'The Boxing Day Shoot', by Julian Tennyson

None of your damp, clammy Christmases this time...but three days of fine sun, a nip in the air, and chill, flaming sunsets. Good shooting weather, and as the birds have been given a rest since the beginning of the month, we have hopes of a Boxing Day well above the average....

Luckily we have been spared any serious frost and snow, so that Johnson, the farmer, has been able to leave two root-fields unpulled without much risk of damage to them. But when, about a fortnight ago, he foresaw a cold sharp spell in the offing, we had some difficulty dissuading him from getting on with the work there and then. So we asked him to shoot on Boxing Day and got round him that way and left him swearing he would have the roots up the moment the shoot was over.

On Boxing Day the same old party is with us, except for an extra gun and beater. My brother and myself, Henton the publican, Fane of the general stores, the Colonel with young Caster considerably improved by a season's strenuous work, and finally farmer Johnson, who, fortunately, loves his bit of shooting and can always be relied to do his best for us by keeping an eye on the state of things at the farm.

The beaters, old Willie the sexton (more bent and more ancient than ever, but still as keen and wily as before), Johnnie the gardener, George the roadman, Harold, one of Johnson's labourers, and young Fane, the storekeeper's son, make up as good a party of men as can be found in the county. They know the land thoroughly, the habits of the birds and how to exploit them, and they are game till the last shot is fired.

So we set off at 10 o'clock in the morning, and conditions seem to be in our favour. There is quite a strong north wind blowing, but this too will help us if anything, for it will keep the birds off that dreaded boundary hedge running along the top side of the shoot. Henton, however, rather damps our ardour by announcing gloomily that the weather forecast last night was 'High wind and rain later'. Very much later, we hope.

This is by no means an easy shoot to drive, although the boundary is fairly straight and the fields on the top side are divided neatly into two strips. We should like to concentrate the birds in the two root fields (they will take to the roots right enough in this weather) but the drawback to the lower 10 acre root field is that the hedges around it are rather sparse and that it will be difficult to drive in any direction as it is almost surrounded by plough. So on second thoughts Henton and I decide that it will be wisest to try to put the birds into the top field and the arable beyond it, though in the latter field they will be perilously near the boundary.

It is easy to make out a plan for shooting beforehand, but extremely difficult to put it into practice, for nearly always some hitch occurs, or else the birds do not go at all where you intend them to. But to-day we should be able to control them reasonably well. Henton and I have the plan worked out to the full — two or three drives (which will take much longer than one would think) on the top side in the morning, and some fun with the pheasants in the 15 acre wood in the afternoon, with another look at the partridges afterwards unless it is too late and we are too exhausted.

There are still any number of birds on the land, for although we have had some sixty brace off it, we have been careful not to shoot it too often. Our driving has not met with much success as yet, and this looks like being the best day for conditions that we have had.

Coming up from the village Henton and I have a talk with old Willie and he agrees with us that it will be best to get the birds going along the top edge of the shoot and leave the fields along the north of the road to more or less look after themselves, and then to drive whatever has gone into the roots and arable in the top corner due southwards, in the hope that the birds will go down on the big arable on the south side of the road.

'Do you think you can manage 'em along the top there, Willie?' asks Henton, rather doubtfully, for it isn't an easy drive at all.

'Course I can,' says Willie, indignantly. 'There's birds on that big arable on the top side that simply *must* fly westwards for they roots. It's their line, Mr Henton and with a wind like this, where else would they go?'

Leave it to Willie. The best beater ever been in the county, as Henton is fond of saying.

So, when we get to the beginning of the shoot, it is all arranged with Willie that the guns shall walk the two big ploughs (heavy going for a start) due westwards, sending (we hope) anything that gets up into one or other of the root fields, and then line the hedge between the 28 acre arable and the plough at the top. When we are ready the beaters will bring the grasses and the big arable straight along towards us. This should be a good drive if things go well, for the big arable is a favourite field, as Willie well knows.

Off we go across the plough, followed by much chaff from the waiting beaters; but the going isn't really bad, for the ground is quite firm.

'Rotten day for scent,' remarks the Colonel, thinking of the possible tasks in store for young Caster (still on the lead), but Henton reminds him of the gloomy weather forecast and says that it won't be so bad when the thaw sets in at midday provided the forecast is right and there is rain ahead.

'The ground's getting soft already, Colonel,' he asserts. 'Get a bit of moisture in it and the scent will be improved no end.'

We don't expect anything of these ploughed fields at this time of the morning, though it is the only kind of day on which the birds might take to them at all.

We stumble along, stepping clumsily on the ridges, and just at the end of the second field four birds rise, when we are still a long way off, and skim lightly over into the lower root-field. At the top corner of the second plough we make our way through a gate and a hedge into the plough above the roots, and here we move very carefully, for the hedge is none too thick and we don't want the birds on the arable to get a warning of our presence before the beaters begin their drive.

Three-quarters of the way up the field there are two trees, some 10 yards apart, which make a set landmark every year for some covey driven off the arable. If the wind is right and their suspicions are not roused, they *will* take that flight, and it is a thing at which old Henton has never ceased to marvel. We are so sure of them taking the line today that we draw lots for the position at the bottom of the field. The luck of the draw is farmer Johnson's.

'Ha!' he shouts, slapping his gaiters gleefully.

'Shut up man!' growls the Colonel sternly. 'If you make a noise like that you won't see 'em at all.'

Not a word as we line the hedge, standing some 10 yards behind it, and presently I blow my whistle as a signal for the beaters to begin. That sound has to carry a long way and I dare not blow too loudly, but in any case old Willie will have his own ideas as to when they should start. It is anxious work, waiting for the driven partridge, straining every nerve to catch the low blast of the whistle or the sudden whirr as a covey rises. It is difficult indeed to control one's excitement so that the shot when it comes is not spoiled.

The minutes drag by without a sound to be heard but the wind sweeping down the hedge in front and Fane spitting lustily, quite a startling noise, upon the plough. Where the devil are the birds? They *must* be up to them by now; I hope to goodness Willie is far enough ahead on the boundary and has got that Coronation handkerchief of his for even with this wind there's no accounting...

Ah! at last. No sooner are the beaters in the arable than *whi-r-r-r, kuk-kuk, kuk-kuk*, a shrill excited whistle, and through the hedge I can just see a fine covey of eight skimming down the field straight between my brother and myself.

The outside bird breasts the hedge; hup! he sees me, and he rises for an instant, half-turning. The perfect shot, but I am too slow with the second barrel and well behind the last bird when they are past me. My brother has also scored a single, a nice broadside, for the birds are coming at the devil of a speed.

Meanwhile the expected covey has taken that never-failing line further up the field, coming splendidly high and very fast indeed. Johnson is rather a wild shot, but he scores one, and Henton makes a real beauty when the birds are well past Johnson and nearly 60 yards away. Even the Colonel's moustache quivers enviously, but not for long, because an old redleg, skimming the hedge, nearly takes his hat off. Barking a sharp Indian oath, the Colonel wheels round in a trice, but surprise has thrown him off his balance, and he doesn't quite get up to the bird.

The beaters are now almost across the field, so that all is clear for Caster to be let loose on Henton's bird, which is running strongly for the top hedge. The Colonel hurries to the spot, and the scent must be fairly good, for Caster picks up a burning line and runs it straight as a die, getting the bird before it has time to find a good hide in the bare hedge.

'Not bad for a start — two brace,' says Fane happily, and we arrange with Willie what the next drive is to be.

There seems nothing for it but to take the lower root-field, by walking it through, hoping that the birds (we know that there are now two coveys in it for certain) will fly to the next roots or the arable below the road, and let the beaters drive the top roots and the arable down to us when we are ready. We *could* have the first root-field driven westwards to us, but a fusillade too near the top root-field would very likely disturb any birds in it, while it is doubtful whether the driven birds would take a line due westward with no cover in front of them.

So the guns set off to walk the roots and the plough above the road, and we flush three coveys in the roots. One breaks up and swerves southwards, some of the birds going high right down to the heath and others bless them! settling in the big arable just south of the road; the second flies straight on across the plough and the stream, going very strongly, too strongly we fear, to stop on the land at all; the third obliges us by making for the top roots.

In this field, however, we have the luck to flush ten pheasants, and two cocks and two hens are shot. One is a beauty, swerving very high right down the line, missed by two people and eventually brought down by Fane. There is one runner, unfortunately, and he gets to the hedge on the road, where all the searching of my old dog Dan fails to find him. Dan has some difficulty in hitting the line at all, for with ten pheasants and three coveys having used the field he hasn't much of a chance. In the hedge the scent seems pretty dead, the bird has probably run a quarter of a mile and may be on the next shoot by now, so after some trying we give it up for lost.

Through the plough we draw a blank, and five of us stay behind the hedge facing the top roots while my brother crosses the stream and faces the arable, to cut off any birds which have a mind to cross the boundary. The whistle is blown and the beaters bring the roots towards us on their first drive.

The wait is not long this time, but the birds have heard the recent firing and seem unwilling to take the flight towards the arable behind us. When we hear a yell from Willie we know that they are trying to break sideways and cross to the lower roots again. He does succeed in turning half the covey by violent use of that famous handkerchief, and the Colonel at the east end gets a fine, high, swinging shot, bringing his bird down stone dead.

One small covey comes just right in the middle of the line, and I manage to scrape one directly behind me. I hate those very low shots when the birds are past. A third covey won't face us at any price; they are redlegs as cunning as cats, and they're off to the west and right across the arable over the boundary. Henton's views on redlegs are unprintable.

When the beaters go back to beating the topmost arable southwards, the guns move along the hedge, so that two cover the roots, two the arable on the near side of the stream, and two on the far side.

Here the birds come over in driblets, and a good many are missed. Johnson gets one. Fane gets another, while Henton and the Colonel confound each other by missing badly with both barrels. Everyone has a say in it, for across the stream both Fane and my brother get shots at a covey which Willie has skilfully headed off the boundary by walking 40 yards in front and making the most uncouth noises and gestures. My brother wings his bird, but Fane's goes unharmed. Never mind; two birds in four makes first class shooting at driven partridges, is Henton's invariable opinion.

My brother's bird is a runner, but it is lovely to see the way old Dan goes to work. With very little scent on the grass he goes straight up-wind and hits the line at once, running it to the hedge on the east side of the field, and almost down to the road. Generously applauded by the Colonel, who realises Caster is better on the end of a lead in a case like this, old Dan has the bird back in under five minutes, after scarcely any hesitation at all and only once over-running the line.

Now it is a quarter to twelve and we have only one more drive before an early lunch. And this one drive, in which we shall try to coerce the birds on the 22 acre arable south of the road, is likely to be the trickiest of the whole day. The obvious line is due northwards, sending the birds back where they came from, but this means driving them straight into the wind, which seems to be freshening every moment. On the other hand, it is hopeless to drive them in any other direction, as we cannot tell what line they would take and are almost bound to lose them. So with some misgivings we arrange to drive northwards after all, and Henton and the Colonel volunteer to walk the hedges at the sides of the field some 60 yards ahead of the beaters, to do their best with any birds which try to break sideways.

The rest of the guns line the hedge on the plough, north of the road, and Henton sets off with the beaters behind the hedge round the east side of the arable. To get behind the west hedge the Colonel takes a short cut through the strip of copse.

There are birds in the arable all right, for almost as soon as the beaters have begun their drive a fine covey rises halfway up the field; but it won't face the wind and goes swirling back high over the beaters' heads down towards the heath. Confound this wind! A second covey of four birds takes a westward line and crossed right in front of the Colonel, rising over the hedge and swinging

down with the wind lifting them. The Colonel downs the leader in grand style, but the pace is too much for him and he is not quick enough in turning for his second barrel. Henton makes short work of a single grey bird skimming eastwards towards the farm and right at the top of the field three redlegs, not feeling the wind until it is too late, top the road-hedge near the corner of the long copse. I miss very badly, but Fane hits his bird hard so that it carries into the stubble behind it, towers suddenly in the wind to a height of 30 yards, and comes down with a slump in the middle of the field. Fane sets off to pick it up and the rest of us make our way towards the farm.

Over a beer-and-sandwich lunch in Johnson's parlour we are agreed that six brace and three pheasants is a commendable effort for a morning's driving. Really the birds behaved quite well, and Henton recalls disastrous days of his youth when in a gale of wind and rain not a single covey would face the guns at all. This reminds the Colonel of a time when he shot quail in a sandstorm in Egypt and the usual volume of stories follows from the repertoires of these two veterans.

By 1.30 we are on the move again, for Henton's weather forecast looks like being correct; it has turned much warmer, the wind is rising and falling ominously and a few black clouds have gathered in the north and east. With luck the weather will not break until we have finished with the pheasants; but driving the wood will take some time, for there is a fine stock left and the cocks are as wily as they could be. We reared about 150 birds in the breeding season and have been feeding regularly on barley rakings, wheat and split maize throughout the winter.

Leaving the farm, we set off southwards down the road, through the gate by the bridge, and begin by walking the marsh and heath straight towards the wood. The marsh is rather bare at this end, but three pheasants are flushed from reed-bed and fly to the wood, none of them offering a shot. It is a favourite place for hares, however, and two, rising well ahead of the line are stopped nicely by Fane and Johnson. Good shots those, for it is a risky business shooting hares nearly out of range, and as likely as not they are simply wounded in the body.

On the heath my brother and Henton and I get three rabbits and a pheasant between us. The heath is thick gorse and scrub and makes very difficult driving; no doubt we have left a good half-dozen pheasants behind us when we came to the wood.

And now the guns line the ride in the centre of the wood, while the beaters, dumping their game-bags on the edge of the grass field, prepare to drive the eastern half towards us. Early this morning I have taken the precaution of lining both sides of the ride with large pieces of paper on sticks and bushes, to try to prevent the birds running out, for run they will at this time of year, especially the cocks, which have learnt all the tricks long before December.

Beating a wood is a very difficult job. The birds have the advantage of the beaters; they run back, they run sideways, they cannot be forced to fly straight ahead unless the line is very close. And the unfortunate beaters often lose sight of each other and get torn to pieces by brambles. The great point is that they should make as much noise as possible (our men produce some truly extraordinary sounds from guttural bellows to high-pitched wails like a huntsman whose voice is breaking!) and hit the trees loudly with their sticks.

The first half of the wood will be driven in two strips, and one gun will remain on the cart-track the whole time to deal with any birds breaking down to the marsh.

Off they go, the dogs are loosed to give them some help, and a medley of sound ensues, terrifying enough to curdle the blood of the stoutest cock-pheasant. No more than two hens are to be shot by each gun. In January hens will be spared altogether, for, as usual, it is the cocks who keep out of harm's way, and if we are not careful we shall find they outnumber the hens by 3 to 1, whereas one cock will suffice for eight hens during the breeding-season.

No sooner have the beaters entered the undergrowth than we can hear the patter of pheasants' feet on the dead leaves as they come running towards the ride. We keep absolutely still, and some run right up to us, pause to look at us for a moment and either run back or fly gently across the ride. The beaters are doing their work well, young Caster is thoroughly enjoying himself, and as far as we can tell not many birds have broken back.

Suddenly comes Johnnie's throaty roar; 'Cock for-ward!' and the old cock pheasant comes hurtling across the wood, right over the trees and travelling at a rare speed. Now the ride is some 20 ft. across and fortunately the trees on either side are thin, so that there is plenty of room for the forward shot — always shoot driven birds in front of you, both pheasants and partridges, if it is possible to do so without danger to the beaters. The bird crashes down in front of Henton, and it is a signal for the fun to begin in earnest, for the pheasants, mostly hens, now come over at all angles, some swerving down over the cart-track, where Johnson has some good shooting, others flying beautifully high and fast or skimming warily across the ride. Some fine shots are missed, for haste in reloading always makes one's aim a bit ragged, and the bag at the end of the drive is six hens and three cocks, with several down in the wood behind us.

Marking shot birds in a wood is a terrible task; the finding of dead birds must generally be left to the dogs en route, while to try to pick up a runner is almost hopeless. A running pheasant can give a partridge 40 yards in a hundred.

When the beaters drive the north part of the wood on the same side of the ride, the fun is not quite so furious, as many of the birds have doubtless made their escape while the lower half was being driven. Only one cock and two hens are shot this time, and so many break out to the north that Henton moves round to the plough to cut some of them off.

However, we are assured of some good sport when we drive the western half of the wood, which the beaters will take, in one part this time, towards the north-west corner. For this there is still one gun on the cart-track, while two are on the plough and three on the grass, standing some 30 yards back from the wood. We know that a certain number of birds are bound to make for the copse on the road.

It is a great drive indeed. Slowly the beaters fight their way through the undergrowth, keeping up a tremendous noise all the time and stopping to look for the fallen birds, while Dan and Caster strike terror into the hearts of skulking old cocks trying to run back unseen.

Again the birds break wildly, coming out of the wood at all points, but most of them steer a course over the north corner, though when they get too high some of them turn with the wind. Some fine shots are given, and again nearly half of them are missed. To the more unpractised eye the pheasant seems to travel so slowly, especially when he is very high up, whereas his speed is in reality much greater than that of either partridge or grouse. During a lull at my end of the line I notice how Henton and the Colonel give themselves plenty of time for each shot, swinging with the bird and continuing their swing even after firing. They put in some fine work between them. The dozen hens have been shot long ago so that all the hens which now leave the wood are allowed to go unharmed.

It is exciting work, requiring fast loading and a very quick eye as the birds come rocketing out of the wood. Each shot makes one tingle with pleasure. In the end the total bag for the wood is 12 hens and 15 cocks; the Colonel says he wishes he could feed his birds and train them like that, and Fane wipes his brow and asserts that he will dream of the last high cock for months to come.

It is well past three o'clock. After a pause to allow the beaters to recover their breath and pick some of the thorns out of their hands, Harold and young Fane are sent on to the farm with as many pheasants as they can carry, while the rest of us prepare to finish the day by driving the long copse and the marsh from west to east.

Henton, Fane, myself and one beater go off to the copse, while the others make their way down to the marsh: the reeds are very thick right down to where the stream crosses from the pond to the river. During the drive, in which both guns and beaters will take part, one gun will walk ahead on the cart-track in case any birds rise well ahead of the line and cross to the wood out of shot.

George and I have a difficult time struggling through the copse. Fane walks the road and Henton the field on the south, whilst I do my best to combine beating with shooting and pick up a few snap-shots between the trees. By the end of it we have got two cocks, but down on the marsh a fusillade of shooting is going on.

'Must be swarms of birds down there,' says Henton wonderingly as we walk down beside the stream. From the grass field we watch the line going through the chest-high reed-beds.

'There go a cock! There go another! Damme, missed'im, and missed'im again. Come on Johnson, he'll be past you. No, no, my boy, too slow. Oh dear, oh dear! There's another one missed.'

It seems that every bird which rises gets away. Old Henton goes off into roars of laughter, laying his gun on the grass and doubling up with his hands on his knees. The Colonel, shaking a fist at him, misses another cock as it rises almost under his feet, and Henton's thunderous laughter goes rolling down across the river.

'There's one on the end of your barrels, Colonel!' he yells. 'Well, I'll be blowed!' he adds. 'Not a man Jack among 'em can touch a bird. What a finish! What a box o' fireworks!'

With that Olympian laughter echoing about their ears, the party down on the marsh comes sheepishly towards us, having accounted for just two pheasants and fired some 25 cartridges.

'Poor light,' says the Colonel gruffly.

'Couldn't see over the reeds,' mumbles Johnson.

But another uncontrolled bellow from Henton sets us all laughing together.

Just at that moment a few drops of rain spatter down out of the leaden sky. We have all forgotten about the weather in the excitement of the chase, and now it looks as if we are in for a real drenching, for the wind has that ominous whistle in it and heavy clouds are rolling overhead,

'That's all for today, sir, eh?' says Henton, turning up his coat collar, and we hurriedly set out for the farm, the beaters collecting their bags and trudging along behind us. It is getting dark now and we are lucky indeed that the weather has held out all day.

Back in the cosy farm-parlour Mrs Johnson sets about brewing enough tea for eleven people and Willie's announcement that the bag is 35 pheasants, 6 brace of partridges, 2 hares and 3 rabbits, makes it taste even better than it is...

This day described by Julian Tennyson, although written just before the 1939 War could as well be written of many rough shoots in the post-war period, right up to the present day. During the Second World War the country as a whole was even more heavily involved than in 1914. Once more farming was of paramount importance in the nation's survival. Once more shooting was a means of providing food rather than a sport, but cartridges were virtually unobtainable. Both gamekeepers and poachers were at war. The nation was fighting shoulder to shoulder for its very existence.

With the end of the war in 1945 came a slow realisation that it was all over at last. As an echo of the previous post-war hysteria there was an almost immediate outbreak of anti-hunting polemics for almost identical reasons based on ignorance of what was involved and possibly also an idealistic desire to interfere with other people's activities. On this occasion a bill was actually put before Parliament with the avowed aim of banning hunting and shooting and ultimately fishing. It had the effect of rallying all supporters of field sports and the bill was handsomely defeated, but the warning had been given.

A sounder piece of legislation, the Protection of Birds Act, proposed in 1947 and passed in 1954, was an overdue measure of control welcomed by all sportsmen and countrymen. By making it a criminal offence to remove eggs from the nests of listed birds, or to shoot the birds themselves, it ended bird and egg-collecting, which though on the wane since Victorian days had reached scandalous proportions and affected the rarer species.

Throughout the 1950s and 60s various trends in Britain affecting sport became apparent. By 1950 the population had exploded beyond the fifty million mark. Each year over 35,000 acres of good agricultural land, the equivalent of about sixty Kensington Gardens and Hyde Parks combined, were being turned over to concrete for new motorways, new towns, or building land. There was estimated to be one car to every twenty-five yards of road in the country. Bad enough in themselves, all these figures were increasing annually with frightening speed.

Due to penal taxation and post-war inflation there was a further break-up of large estates which had survived the First World War. There was also an increased interest in rough-shooting, without the expense of a keeper or organized beaters. German Shorthaired Pointers, the pointer-retrievers used in Germany, were brought back by returning ex-servicemen and found useful on unkeepered ground where there was little game.

In the 1950s the German Shorthaired Pointers were the first new breed of gundog recognized by the Kennel Club since the Yellow Labrador nearly forty years before. The categories for gundog breeds were still unchanged since the turn of the century, namely pointers and setters, retrievers and spaniels. In recognising German Shorthaired Pointers 'and those breeds which hunt, point and retrieve', the Kennel Club was in effect recognising a fourth category of gundog, the pointer-retriever. The wheel had turned full circle since the early nineteenth century when every gundog was expected to point and retrieve.

From a sporting viewpoint the introduction of myxomatosis was the major event of the 1950s. In 1953 the disease spread from France and, although contained to some extent until 1954, thereafter it spread rapidly throughout the country. This was a disease deliberately developed in the laboratory with a view to killing a particular animal, but the truly frightening feature of it was that it was initially spread accidentally by a French scientist who merely wished to rid his own small estate of rabbits.

No one who has observed the effects of the disease at close quarters in the countryside can avoid the unpleasant question in their mind as to what might happen should the disease mutate and attack humans, or other animals. Admittedly the rabbit was a great pest and some means of control was urgently required. It was said the rabbit trapping industry and subsidiaries, worth an estimated 15 million pounds, were ruined and agriculture benefited by an estimated 50 million pounds annually — although both these figures are subject to the usual dubiety such rough estimates always arouse. More important in the long run perhaps, the countryside was rent with bitterness and ill-feeling between those who favoured the spread of the disease and those who loathed it.

With the introduction of cheaper shotguns from Spain, from the USSR and from the USA, as well as the staggering increase in the number of cars during the 1960s and 1970s shooting, at game and also at clay pigeons, increased enormously in popularity. Nowhere was now too isolated to be visited if desired. Poaching with silenced .22s and telescopic sights was all too common. On the foreshore there were too many 'marsh cowboys'. The registration of shotguns became inevitable and in 1968 an act was passed making this law.

During the 1970s and 1980s all these influences began to coalesce. Farming was still booming. Farmers were disinclined to lease shooting, preferring either to keep it for themselves, or demand an increasingly high price. At the same time game-rearing was being developed to a very high degree, so that one man could easily rear several thousand birds. The pressures on shooting and the shooting ground available were immense and steadily increasing.

Some idea of shooting in the late fifties and early sixties may be had from the following extracts from 'Short Days from a Roughshooter's Diary' extracted from *The Roughshooter's Sport.*

November 5th

I went out with George for a couple of hours this afternoon. Although we have often shot together this was the first time he had shot over the dogs. As he had often expressed interest and scepticism I was disappointed when he announced on arrival that he felt as if he had flu. He looked ill, but insisted obstinately in going out and bringing his old black labrador, June. She is usually firmly shackled to his waist, but now he wanted to let her go. I pointed out, mildly, that it was not much use working the dogs in front if she ran through all their points, so, somewhat reluctantly, he agreed to keep her on the lead.

The dogs started off by pointing a cock pheasant in a small patch of roots in front of him. He made the common mistake of those shooting over pointing dogs for the first time and fired much too soon, missing with both barrels. Fortunately I was able to down it with the choke barrel satisfactorily. It was then retrieved on command by Max.

We then moved on to take the roadside strip, with one gun each side and the dogs in the middle; fat June panting heavily in the rear. Half-way down the strip George shot a partridge which rose ahead of him, but it was an obvious runner. He called June and set her on to it and, rather to my surprise, she found the scent at once and started off with her head down going strongly.

Mistakenly thinking she was running wild he tried to call her off, but, quite rightly she paid no attention and went on to find the bird and bring it back, somewhat chewed. Quite a good piece of work for her.

I could not afford to be critical, however, for a moment or two later Max flushed a cock pheasant and I missed a simple crossing shot with both barrels. It then rocketed over the tree tops and George brought it down, as it started to curl, with a beautiful shot that crumpled it in mid-flight. Max started to run forwards and had to be checked firmly. June then went forwards instead and picked the bird. Unfortunately she decided to take it into a field of thick kale and when she returned to George, after repeated whistling, she no longer had it with her.

'We'll never find that now,' swore George.

'Don't be too sure of that,' I replied. 'Hie lost, Max.'

Perhaps June had not taken it far. Anyway, to my relief and satisfaction, and to George's, he appeared with it almost at once. There after there was a subtle change in George's attitude. Admittedly he expressed doubts when Max was seen, having been sent for a runner, galloping at full speed along the edge of the boundary wall, nearly a quarter of a mile away.

'He's gone wild, hasn't he?' he asked.

'No. He's got it,' I replied.

Sure enough, he had. And on his return with the wing tipped bird, still very much alive in his jaws, George was profuse in his praise. Even when Werra, coming from downwind, flushed a covey of partridges out of range, he expressed no irritation. But it was obvious he was feeling far from well and his shooting was suffering, so we soon turned for home. At least he was able to retire to bed with some pleasant memories, or, in spite of everything, we managed to collect three and a half brace of pheasants, a partridge and a hare between us.

Verdict. Not without amusement. June would probably have been quite good with more practice.

November 7th

John came over unexpectedly, full of his usual nautical aplomb and assurance. He arrived just as I was due to go to an appointment, but, intent on having a shot at something, he suggested, with the coolness which characterizes him, that he should 'borrow' one of the dogs. I explained, as patiently as possible, that I did not think either of them would work for anyone else. However he was not to be deterred and, after some discussion, I eventually let him have Werra on a lead, much to her obvious disgust.

He had hardly reached the end of the drive before, as I had expected, she had slipped her collar and returned to me. But John is nothing if not persistent. 'Taking another reef in her collar' as he expressed it, he led her off again. This time he was nearly two hundred yards away before she did exactly the same thing. I suggested again that he might give it up, but he insisted on trying once more. This time we had started the car and were moving off when she re-appeared without John. Opening the car door we let her in and drove off.

Moral. Don't trust sailors with your girl, or your dog. A good dog should only work for its owner.

Left to himself, John returned happily with three rabbits and in the afternoon I took him up to the moor to demonstrate the workings of the kite hawk, in which he had expressed airy disbelief. To begin with I had difficulty with what he naturally termed the 'moorings'. I suspect the children have been playing with it. In any case it took some time to prepare and, with an indifferent breeze, I had quite a job getting it to rise. Finally, after several false starts and nose dives, it was airborne.

John was just beginning to express disbelief again when he all but trod on a covey sitting tight and they exploded in all directions. His right and left could scarcely have been improved upon and a few minutes later the dogs had retrieved the birds to hand.

'It works,' John admitted, in surprised tones.

'It not only works, but it's your turn to work it,' I replied.

But the wind was fluky and, for all that he was a Fleet Air Arm pilot, John was unable to keep it up for long. Nor was I able to do any better when I took over again. We managed to get another brace and a half of grouse and a brace of partridges on the lower ground, but finally a particularly vicious nose dive to earth broke one of the struts and finished our sport for the day.

Final bag. Two and a half brace of grouse, one brace of partridges and three rabbits. Memo. Mend kite.

November 7th

Another cold day with a blustery east wind. I went out via the trap round in the Howkins and found another stoat in the same tunnel trap which has caught two weasels and a rat in the past fortnight. It is obviously a main trunk road and such main junctions are well worth knowing. At the extreme end of the wood there were a couple of crows feasting on a rabbit carcass. I managed to shoot the nearest with the choke barrel before they were out of range. Max retrieved it and I decided to use it as a decoy. Propped on a stick by the rabbit it looked quite realistic. Having waited ten minutes in the wood I was about to give it up when another crow appeared. Although it circled suspiciously, it came within range and was also successfully downed. The question is whether it was the companion to the one already shot?

I then went past the Hairy Crag. What lovely local names places have. Thence down to the river where a teal rose and was promptly shot. It planed down steadily and I could have sworn crossed the river. But when Max was sent forward he barely had to get his feet wet and it was stone dead. Which just goes to show how astonishingly deceptive to shoot and mark teal are after mallard. There may be nothing original in that but it is easily forgotten. They appear to be further away because they are so small, whereas geese appear to be closer because they are much larger.

I waited for duck, but only heard a faint whicker of wings. A family of owls in the woods opposite managed to sound like a troop of boy scouts on the rampage. Patrol Owl. Anyone who thinks the country is quiet ought to listen to owls. They'd be glad to get back to the quiet of the big city where the mice and rats only have to worry about cats.

Bag. Two crows, one teal, three shots.

November 14th
A bright sunny morning. I took an hour off with the old hammer gun to pick up a rabbit. I started by walking up the mound to the gorse bushes behind the house, where rabbits can usually be found. There was a lot of *chissicking* of partridges audible and I knew there must be a covey sunning themselves in the gorse. I duly sent Max in and a covey rose at once as I expected. Having had plenty of time to cock the hammers and make ready I took a right and left from it. I set Max on to the retrieving and he promptly retrieved a runner, but missed the other lying stone dead in the gorse. Instead he started moving forwards fairly fast on an obvious scent. Not realising it was not another runner I encouraged him and he promptly flushed another covey which must have been lying beside the first. Although reloaded I had no time to cock, or even to take a snap shot before they were over the slope of the hill and safe. It was my fault for encouraging him to go forwards. I sent him back and he promptly retrieved the dead bird.

He then retired of his own volition and came on a firm point at a tuft of grass. On command he moved on a large healthy rabbit, which I rolled over stone dead a moment or two later. The object of the outing having thus been concluded I made a detour back to the house via a neighbouring field of roots. A fine cock was duly flushed and brought down stone dead as it rose to cross the hedge. The brief larder filling was thus eminently successful.

Although the bag was satisfactory it should have been larger had I been awake. It would be tempting to blame the hammer gun, but that did not really have anything to do with it. I might just have got off one doubtfully effective snap shot with a hammerless gun, but, had I been alive to the fact that there was another covey present, as I should have been, I would have been ready with any type of gun.

One cock pheasant, a brace of old partridges, one rabbit. Four shots.

November 16th

It was a cold and blustery morning with the sun trying to come through at intervals. I tried the Howkins, via the Hairy Crag, with disastrous results. To start with I had five abortive shots at rabbits in the gorse patches. (Could it be that I got those cartridges damp the other day? However, that shouldn't make all that much difference. The unavoidable conclusion is that it must just be me.) Finally a cock pheasant flushed above the wood rocketed upwards, curling deceptively in the wind, but I put both barrels into the air somewhere close to it. It was certainly a pricked bird and came down, planing slowly, almost at the other end of the wood. I put Werra on to it and she went off at speed, following the trail down the edge of the wood to the cottage, a hundred yards, or more, farther on. She was obviously at a loss here, so I called her off and set Max on. He followed the same line and then cast around and swung left, parallel to the road, for a couple of hundred yards above the Castle. He was obviously at fault here, but cast around again and crossed the road. He found the scent again almost at once, so obviously the bird had still been able to fly after a fashion and had crossed the sunken road there.

He cleared the wall above the Castle and here he really started to move at a gallop downhill towards the river. He was soon out of my sight, though I had been following hard. He was already well over half a mile from where the bird had been shot. But presently he returned to view, the old darling, with the cock held in his jaws. It was only wing-tipped and had spurs on it like a Mexican cowboy. It had certainly done its best, but with an intelligent and determined dog on its trail it had met its match. What a pleasure it was to watch that piece of work. It shows the difference between an experienced dog and an inexperienced one, as I think Werra's nose is just about as good as Max's. She just does not have the experience yet.

After that anything else would have been bound to be pure anti-climax, however I was inspired to take a high flying black-backed gull with the choke barrel on the way home.

Sum total for the day, eight shots for one black-backed gull and one cock pheasant which certainly wouldn't have graced the bag but for Max. Verdict. Poor shooting, but the day redeemed by a wonderful piece of dog work.

November 20th

A cloudy day without much sun, but warmer with a strong west wind. M., a friend from Florida, came out with me. To begin with, walking downwind, we flushed some coveys out of range. Then Max came on point on M's left. On command he flushed two pheasants, one rather immature. M took the mature

bird well and dropped him in the stubble. After that we saw no more game until we reached the end of the hill, where a big buck hare got up on my right. I gave him the choke barrel at long range and saw him check, but he went on up the hill strongly.

At the top of the first incline he stopped and looked back, so I sent Max after him. As soon as he saw Max, he turned and vanished at speed. In a moment or two Max was also out of sight following the scent strongly. We neither of us thought, as we admitted afterwards, that he had much chance, but we waited at the foot of the hill for ten minutes and then, sure enough, Max appeared again, still at the gallop, with the hare in his jaws. Although hit in the lungs it must have travelled a long way before finally expiring.

When we turned into the wind on the boundary field Max came on a firm point. Werra came up and backed him. One old partridge and one surprisingly young, almost a cheeper, were flushed. I took aim on the cheeper and then switched to the old bird. M and I fired simultaneously. The old bird dropped dead, probably rather heavy with shot. Both of us were apologetic. Technically it may have been my bird, but it should have been left to the guest. To redeem matters Max then pointed a cock pheasant, which flew boundarywards and was nicely downed by M.

We then worked a field of late stooks, somewhat waterlogged. The dogs flushed a hare, which M took neatly with a well placed shot. Finally we waited for duck until five thirty and had one shot at the sole mallard to come over, but it was too high.

Verdict. A very pleasant afternoon's sport even if not much was shot. One partridge, one brace of pheasants, two hares. Plenty of game seen. M's description of the dog work was: 'Mighty useful dawgs. Bird dawgs, hare dawgs, rabbit dawgs, water dawgs, every sort of dawgs.' High praise.

November 30th

Cold and windy day, but having just built a new platform in the top wood I decided to try it out. I fixed one very indifferent and rather drunken-looking pigeon to a pole and set it up to one side of the hide. The position is an excellent one with an all-round field of fire and the birds' flight naturally there, but still the sport was better than I had expected. I fired off fifty cartridges and the final pick-up was twenty-one pigeons. However one or two are definitely stuck up in the trees as is almost always the way when firing from a platform like that. There are probably one or two farther out round the wood too. But, even so, that wasn't bad, considering the way they were curling in the wind. That is certainly a good hide. It does, however, need re-inforcing. There is a weak spot in one corner which nearly caused me to descend thirty feet head first. It was just as well I built a side rail round it. Also it could be easier to get into. I must see what I can do to improve it.

Verdict. 21 pigeons. 50 shots fired. A very good hour or so.

December 11th

Periodically rainy. Wet and cold. There was nothing in the traps. When I was out for exercise in the afternoon I saw a hare, a couple of hundred yards downwind of me in a bare grass field, catch my scent as I entered the field. It jinxed out of its form, doubled back on its tack and having pranced round three or four times to confuse the scent it finally settled down in another tuft about thirty yards farther on. It approached the final spot with a tremendous sideways jump. I was interested to see what the dogs would make of this, so I held them in until I reached the place where the hare had started its game. On getting the scent they were obviously interested and confused by her backtracking tactics. Before they could fully work it out, however, the hare got up and, as I wanted a hare for the larder, I shot it at full range. Felt a brute.

Verdict. One hare. One shot. Ashamed of myself. No real reason for this as it was a perfectly sporting shot, but on analysing it I decided that, having watched the whole performance the hare had gone through somehow established a personal relationship between us in my mind, so that it was not quite the usual impersonal business. In a way too I suppose I felt I was taking an unfair advantage, cheating, if you like, having seen her elaborate preparations to avoid discovery. An interesting ethical question.

December 16th

A frosty morning with a hint of snow. I set off about eleven to get a brace of pheasants as Christmas presents. Almost at once a covey was flushed behind the hill. I followed them up and flushed them again out of the gorse. One stayed too long, foolish bird, and was pointed efficiently by Max. I took it at long range and it dropped, a strong runner, after flighting downhill for about a hundred yards. I sent Werra after it and she took the wind very sensibly and, making a quick sweep, promptly picked it and brought it to hand well.

Max then pointed a hen pheasant in the hedge just as I was climbing the fence. I sent Werra to flush it on the other side and took it stone dead in the field of roots. Max retrieved it well and quickly to order. I then turned into the wood and the dogs soon flushed a cock pheasant which rocketed upwards through the trees. I took a quick snap shot through the branches into the sun and could have sworn I was on him, but he disappeared going strongly. I marked the direction and followed up. For a first cast I tried the hedge on the far side of the old road, nearly three hundred yards distant. Werra pointed firmly and, on being ordered to flush, came out, instead, with the cock, nicely retrieved. It had been hit in the body, behind.

I then went back via the water splash and flushed a pair of mallard from it. I took the drake cleanly and it turned out to be the fattest mallard I have ever seen. Weight four pounds. I returned late for lunch with the brace of pheasants and one mallard for four shots.

Verdict. My shooting was poor, but the dogs worked well and made up for what it lacked.

December 17th

I went out in the evening. It was blowing a cold wind from the east. While going round the traps I shot a crow and followed it up with two pigeons as I went down to the river to wait for duck. The moor hens were making a lot of noise, but heard duck further up the river and presently they came over low. I took one out of them very satisfactorily and it landed with a thud stone dead on the far side of the river, but missed clean with my second barrel. For a long time no more appeared. Then I heard some farther up the river again. After calling them I heard a noisy drake reply. Presently they appeared on the water at my feet swimming enquiringly down the river with the current. As soon as I moved they were off with a startled *Quark*. I just managed to get one against the sky as they rose and it landed in the water with a loud splash. I sent Max in after him and then over to fetch the other from the far bank. They were both drakes. Nice, plump birds.

Verdict. I cheated abominably and had no excuse for not having a right and left from the first lot. It is interesting, however, that I had no feelings of guilt at calling the duck down the river and I had quite a lengthy conversation with the noisy drake who kept answering my call. The answer, I suppose, is that this was perfectly fair, in that I imitated the duck sufficiently well to deceive it,

whereas with the hare the other day I had watched it go to ground and knew where it was despite its precautions.

Bag. One crow, two pigeons, two mallard, six shots.

December 15th

A strong, gale force wind. I set a trap in a likely hole as I started out, but the birds were almost unshootable. I fired seven cartridges and killed one partridge after tramping round for an hour. The dogs were fed up with it and so was I. It would have been wildfowling weather if it was only colder. On my return I found a weasel dead in the trap I had set earlier. All the others were unsprung.

Verdict. One partridge, seven shots, Lucky to get that and stupid to try.

December 30th

There was a strong freeze up during the night. The sun was a blood red ball in the sky and altogether it was a brisk sort of morning. Max and I started off to walk the hedgerows. Almost at once he came on point and then drew on along the old road. He drew on strongly, obviously on a pheasant, and I followed at speed for some distance. Eventually he put up a cock pheasant, which rose into the sun. I fired a long range crossing shot and brought him down stone dead. Max then retrieved him to hand and I found it was almost an albino. It was certainly one of the most beautiful cocks I have ever seen, probably a Reeves, or Silver, cross. They are reputed to be impossible to walk up and great wanderers and it had certainly been a long and fast chase. However Max coming on point again put an end to reflection.

On command he flushed a covey which had been lying tight against the hedge in the way they often do in frosty conditions. I took an outside bird with each barrel. One stone dead and the other a runner. I sent Max after it, but it was a strong runner and reached the hedge. Every time he nearly reached it the bird wriggled through the hedge again. But eventually he had it and brought it to hand. Good for the old dog.

I followed this by missing a hare with both barrels after it had been duly pointed and flushed. I sometimes wonder if there is any shot in the cartridges. It is that sort of thing and pigeons in a high wind, or curling partridges, that brings down the average of kills to cartridges. But it is a pernicious thing to keep a record of anyway and it is certainly not worth paying any attention to it. The only answer is to take everything that is reasonable and sporting and to disregard the misses. At the same time it is important not to risk wounding game for nothing. But that is enough moralising. Beautiful pheasants are not shot every day, but each shot in itself should be a thing of beauty.

Verdict. One beautiful cock pheasant and a brace of partridges for five shots. Enough beautiful thoughts for today.

During the 1950s and '60s the German Shorthaired Pointers were increasing in popularity and this record of the training of an apparently incurably gun-shy bitch, entitled 'Diary of an Ex-Policewoman or Old Fail-Me-Never', is in the main extracted from *The Roughshooter's Dog,* the first book in the English language on training Pointer-Retriever gundogs and still in print.

I was at Crufts, on the only occasion I have attended that famous dog show, when I was approached by two men identically dressed in grey trilbies and belted mackintoshes. The one who approached me introduced himself as a Chief Inspector, with a sergeant accompanying him. My heart sank as I tried to think of any sins I had committed recently to account for this unlikely visitation. Had I parked my car on some hallowed territory or unwittingly committed some other offence. Their next words relieved my mind.

'We are in charge of the dog training establishment at Biggin Hill,' explained the Chief Inspector. 'We'd like to use your dog as a Sire.'

They went on to explain that Fredrika, Max's litter sister, had greatly impressed them with her scenting abilities. She had tracked a burglar from the scene of the crime to a trolleybus stop through crowded streets. The handler had proposed trying each trolleybus stop to see if he could pick up the trail again. This had been regarded as a forlorn hope, but four stops further on Fredrika had picked up the trail and eventually led her handler to the burglar's house. After that they had decided to breed from her, but the mating had not been very successful and they only had one pup. Regretfully I had to tell them that after a severe attack of hard pad Max, although a powerful male in every respect, was probably sterile. However I was invited to go to Biggin Hill to see over the establishment the following day and was duly impressed by Fredrika, the only dog allowed free range without a lead. I also saw her pup and liked the look of her at nine months, mentioning that if they ever decided to pass her on that I was interested. I was assured that they never sold their dogs. However nine months later I had a telephone call from the Chief Inspector letting me know that the bitch was available as she had proved to be gun-shy and therefore useless for police work. They offered her to me and I agreed to take her as long as they could catch the one o'clock train leaving Euston, on which my wife was travelling. They promptly held the train while a police car with siren pulsing raced across London. The following is a diary of Fredrika II's training:

Saturday 15th December
I met my wife and Fredrika II off London train. Both were somewhat distrait. F II had been in such a nervous condition that every noise of the train had caused her to stand on her head behind my wife's back to the detriment of her suit. Feelings were strained. It was fortunate, however, that they were able to travel together, as I hate to think what would have happened if F II had been travelling in the luggage van alone. She is a complete bundle of nerves. I have never seen a grown dog as flabby, fat and out of condition. She looks as if she is in pup. Her pads are as soft as a young pup's. Obviously she has had no real exercise for some time and has at the same time been too well fed on a rich Metropolitan police diet of steaks and sirloins. The slightest noise such as striking a match is liable to send her literally up the wall, or else round in frantic circles to find a place to hide her head. She looks like being a problem.

However I had no time this evening to do more than feed her a small meal and let her get settled in the kennel. I will take her out tomorrow and see if we can find a suspected cock runner left from today's covert shooting.

Sunday 16th December

Poor old F. I took her out gently over the fields and had to lift her over walls and ditches as she is far too fat and out of condition to cope with them. She obviously did not know how to begin to do so. Having clapped my hands at her I noticed that she tried to run away the first time and then looked up to see what it was all about. I did not believe she was really gun-shy; just gun nervous and everything else nervous. When we reached the area where the cock had been marked Werra came on point almost at once. The cock was flushed on order. I fired a shot at it, watching F., and missed. F. took off and disappeared. Knowing she could not jump a fence, or wall, I went in search of her and found her at last, wandering round vaguely. Meanwhile Werra returned with the cock, which she had retrieved without assistance from me. In the afternoon I took F. out on check lead and fired another shot, to which she did not object unduly. Undoubtedly she is only gun nervous. But out of condition. It will be a six months job just to get her fit.

Monday 17th December

In the late afternoon I took the dogs out and concentrated on trying to get F. to sit on command. She ran away, but Werra joined in and showed her how. Very primly. On the check lead she behaves perfectly, but off it she behaves just as she pleases. I did not fire a shot, as I only saw one pigeon in the darkening, but all the same, I am sure she is much happier already. She is a clear case of arrested development, due to always having been in a kennel and never having been seriously taught anything at all, or having anyone really taking a personal interest in her. She loathes anything flapping, e.g. washing on the line. She will start at the slightest noises, if unexpected, but is already better than she was. She obviously needs some home life and fun and games. She will probably retrieve all right, as the first thing she did on seeing hens was to run in and seize one. She gripped it by the neck and would not bring it to me. She ran off determinedly and I had to get her cornered, hold her, and give her a few strokes with the check lead while holding the fluttering hen in front of her. Fortunately the hen was quite unhurt. I think this treatment may have cured her but hope it doesn't affect her retrieving. I only want to stop her chasing hens. We can't have that, but it doesn't seem to have worried her.

I am certain she is putting on this nervous appearance as she enjoyed mock retrieving with the dummy in the house; running back to her basket and being intercepted before she could chew it. I am cutting down her food to try and get her waistline back. She is disgustingly fat and out of condition. However, she may make a good gundog yet. The mistake I made today was to have her on the check lead beside me. Once off it she tried to stay to heel consistently and refused to roam. She is probably easily tired, but this could very quickly

become a bad habit and I must get her out hunting. I will have to risk letting her run in an chase, in order to get some original bitch in her. This is clearly a case where orthodox measures would be useless.

Tuesday 18th December

I took the three dogs out in quest for a hare and a rabbit. Almost at once we flushed a hare downwind in the grass field below the hill. Fredrika was with me and ran in after it. I shot it cleanly before she could get near it with her ridiculous waddle. Max retrieved it and she made an abortive nibble at it as he brought it back. In the next field Werra drew on well on a trio of partridges running ahead. I took one stone dead and she retrieved well to order. After some more wanderings in growing darkness I fired two abortive barrels at a rabbit, which Werra pointed well, but which Fredrika spoiled by running in through the point. The rabbit lives to run another day. If it is the same one I have persecuted this season in that drain I must have now fired at it at least seven or eight times. What a confession, its pants must be almost armour plated by now.

The verdict on Fredrika is that she is certainly not gun-shy. She embraced my leg and leaped up after most shots to seek reassurance, but gave that up latterly and the run-in after the hare and the rabbit probably did her some good, though both were quite abortive as she is too fat to do much. However I let her climb over walls and through fences as best as she could and she is slowly learning her way about. At present with that absurd weight to carry she is so soft she can't hope to jump much and her pads are obviously itching a lot after the unaccustomed stubble. She is also tired out. The answer is that for a neurotic bitch work is the remedy. Psychologists in Harley Street would no doubt often like to prescribe the same thing. She is no longer gun-shy and is far less nervous. She is sleeping well in spite of noise. She is showing signs of house training as she is a naturally clean dog.

She may be difficult to teach to retrieve and she shows no sign of pointing at all yet, but that and the hunting instinct ought to come fairly soon. She might have quite a gentle mouth if she can be stopped from chewing. At the moment she chews anything and everything just like a teething pup. She certainly ought to point easily enough. She uses her nose a lot, but has a cold which can't help. At the moment I am concentrating on getting her to sit when told. Basic obedience must come first. After she is fully obedient to the command 'Sit' I will go on. If she builds up muscle and is kept hungry she should work all the more willingly for a few bribes. On the whole I feel she might make a gundog yet and am certainly not in despair. It might be a very long job as she is slow to learn, but she does try to help and co-operate and, being conscious of her antecedents, one can't blame her unduly. She might turn out surprisingly well, once she is fully developed mentally and physically.

She must learn to obey at a distance first above all. Today I did my best at intervals to rub this in and feel she would have tried to keep up with the others, but she was so tired she stuck close to heel most of the time and was even underfoot in an annoying fashion. She looked quite hurt when I tried to move her on. However she has essentially an easy and helpful nature, I feel, under her neurosis and flabbiness.

Wednesday 19th December

I shot a hare going steeply uphill in front of Fredrika. It got up at her feet and rolled back in full view of her nerve-kicking, although stone dead. She half stiffened into a point as she watched it. Werra also sat watching it roll back past her. Good training for both of them.

Friday 21st of December

We walked round the foot of the hill. Werra came on point at the fence and Fredrika lumbered up, still unmuscled, and came on her first near point at the sight of Werra. Tail out, body straight and leg up, backing for about five seconds. At least this proves the instinct is there. She is still gamely trying to follow the others and does seem to be coming on quite rapidly, all things considered. She is not in the least frightened now really. At least compared with her immediate arrival. I did not shoot all day, but tested her in the shallow water by the islands. She did not show signs of fright at first, but came on, after some encouragement, and waded belly deep quite cheerfully. Yesterday she fell in up to her waist, but today was quite deliberate and after her first misery she took to it quite cheerfully. She has longer hair than the other two, but seemed to dry off quite well.

Monday 8th January

Fredrika, who obstinately refused to pick the dummy earlier today, went and retrieved a hare on a blind retrieve in gorse, and did it very well. She has a phobia about the dummy and I suspect the police tried to make her pick it and she now has a reaction to it. I will have to take her gently, or could ruin her now. She picked a hare later on today, but would not bring it to hand. Must not force the pace unduly. All her training will have to be at her speed and as the needs of the moment indicate, as she is too old to train on normal lines. She backed Werra well on point, but so far has not had a genuine point of her own. All the time however her instincts are growing stronger. She should be good one day.

Tuesday 9th January

We walked round the boundaries towards the hill. Fredrika had a point of her own and, when I did not immediately follow it up, flushed a hen pheasant. A pity I was not up with her. It was a good point. Max then flushed a cock pheasant out of the wood unexpectedly over my shoulder. I took a snap shot at long range and saw it plane down. On a hunch I followed it up and Werra came on point. Then she flushed the cock over the river and I made no mistake this time. It landed stone dead on the far bank. I sent Max into the water and he leaped in eagerly. After a second's hesitation Fredrika followed him and by the time he reached the bird it was neck and neck. Fortunately she did not try to seize the bird but followed him back with every sign of wishing to do so. In a way it would have been interesting to see if she would have retrieved it. She would obviously retrieve from water itself, which is most illuminating as she is distinctly showing signs of being difficult about retrieving now. Perhaps I have been pushing her too hard. She has obviously been mishandled with a dummy at some time and quivers with fright when asked to retrieve it, or rather when it is put in her mouth, as she will not even pick it up now. This is silly as a few days ago she was willing to fetch it after a fashion. However she is now in season and this may not be helping much. Probably it is partly that.

I can see why the police got tired of her. She can be quite infuriating. I must be careful not to handle her roughly in any way however, although the temptation is very great when she acts, and that is the operative word, stupid on a subject she is known to understand perfectly well. This is a real test of patience. Everything else is easy compared to trying to teach something to an animal apparently scared of lessons. The mind seems to be gripped by the fear of some happening in the past and nothing functions at all, although quite a good mind in practice. The answer with her at the moment would appear to be to leave dummy training well alone and concentrate on giving her plenty of outside retrieving and work. She did a second point on her own today, on a hole. It was confirmed by Werra. Presumably a rabbit. Later she did some nice backing. Only the retrieving appears to be suffering at the moment.

Wednesday 10th January

Fredrika mouthed a partridge, but did not retrieve it. No real damage done fortunately, either to the partridge, or to her. I hope.

Thursday 11th January

Fredrika is now definitely much fitter. She careered away after a hare and retrieved an old mangy specimen of rabbit to hand after mouthing it. She is muscling up now and beginning to get at least some idea of being a gundog.

Friday 12th January

On the hilltop we moved a hare which Fredrika promptly chased. From my position above her I bowled it over cleanly and Fredrika retrieved it to hand well. Not too bad considering that earlier today she refused to fetch the dummy at all. She is obviously windy of any training, but enjoys work. She set off after another hare. The time is approaching for use of check cord.

Sunday 14th January

Today Fredrika twice ran in and seized a rabbit from Werra and brought them to hand after mouthing. Yet this evening she would not retrieve on dummy at all. Nor unfortunately will she run in on the check cord as she feels she is on the lead. Altogether a difficult animal. However this was more or less what was expected. She is just not behaving in the same way twice running, so that it is difficult to work out any reasons for her actions and to work out counters.

Tuesday 16th January

Today I decided Fredrika is merely putting on a neurotic act. She will not retrieve the dummy and I feel the time has come when drastic methods must be applied, since nothing else appears to work.

Wednesday 17th January.

I started today by tying the dummy in F's jaws. A couple of pieces of string were tied round the dummy and joined behind her head. Then I put her on the check lead and led her round for ten minutes. To begin with she was the picture of misery, shivering with fear, mostly pretence, and could not have looked more abject. After five minutes she cheered up and after ten minutes was walking happily beside me, wagging her tail. She would sit and come with it when called. I untied the dummy and she still retrieved perfectly with no attempt at mouthing. In the afternoon I shot a hare and she ran in and mouthed badly, and would not retrieve. What a dog. I must be forcing the pace too hard. One thing at a time. The dummy first and check cord to stop her running in next. I only hope I can get her to run in with it on and bowl her over. She should not need it more than once,

Friday 19th January

Today I tied the dummy in Fredrika's mouth once more. Again it worked perfectly and she carried it without strings for a short period before delivering it to hand without mouthing.

Saturday 20th January

The previous training has now paid off. She is carrying the dummy well, without attempting to mouth, or make any protest. The next stage is getting her to pick it up and retrieve it. She is very close to this, but I must not make the mistake of forcing the pace. She ran in after a hare and disappeared over the hill. She came back dead lame and suspect a greenstick fracture. Perhaps this will teach her. But I doubt it. I will now have to take her gently for a week or so.

Sunday 28th January

She is now retrieving the dummy perfectly without hesitation and enjoying doing so. There is no attempt at mouthing. This makes training much easier. Although her leg is now better she is showing less sign of wanting to run in, so perhaps she did learn something after all.

Friday 2nd February

I laid a trail for Fredrika today, which she followed quite well and retrieved the hare at the end of it extremely well. She is now coming on in leaps and bounds.

Saturday 3rd February

I spoke too soon. Fredrika reverted to mouthing. She made a complete nonsense of the retrieve of a hare. Better to draw a veil over today.

Sunday 4th February

Fredrika is now pointing very well. She is extremely stylish and obviously has a very good nose. The only thing she lacks is experience. If I can now get her retrieving really well and get her completely steady she will be likely to make a really good dog.

Wednesday 28th February

Fredrika caught and ate a rabbit while I was laying traps today. I made her retrieve the hind legs, which were all that was left. She did this perfectly without mouthing. Then refused to retrieve another she had pointed, which I shot. However I put it down and made Werra mark it and retrieve it in full view of Fredrika. Then she did it perfectly. It is surprising what a little example, combined with jealousy, can do. She still bumbles about a lot, instead of quartering well, but she has come on really remarkably well considering the mess she was. She points very well and backs excellently and her retrieving is coming on very reasonably. Also she is a lot steadier.

Sunday 11th March

Fredrika retrieved a jay well. She is now retrieving anything to order, with the minimum of mouthing. In fact she has a gentle mouth as I always suspected and does try to please. She is now almost reliably steady, although full of life and go.

Sunday 18th March

I took F out alone. She quartered reasonably, if erratically. She pointed two rabbits, which were shot over her and both retrieved to order, without attempting to run in. She can be said to be partially trained now.

Tuesday 20th March

Fredrika retrieved a crow very well indeed. She is now beginning to be reliable and only needs to improve her quartering.

Friday 20th April;

Fred put up her last black today, I hope. She chased a sheep in the field. I took her straight off to the pen where the old rams were being held and let them butt her unmercifully. I doubt if she will ever look at a sheep again.

The following month she entered her first Field Trial. She was taken down to London by car and, perforce, spent most of the day without exercise. The following morning, rising at five-thirty, I gave her a two-hour run in the country, when she began to show signs of waking up a little, but barely answered the whistle to start with at all. With some misgivings I took her to the Field Trial. In the morning she ran very badly, but there was little game for her to point, in fact she neither saw nor missed any, but quartered very badly. In the afternoon she woke up in the second stake and quartered very well indeed, but again had no game to point. However she was the only dog to succeed in what was described by the judge as 'a difficult retrieve for the very best dog one might think of'. She did it twice without undue encouragement, whereas only one other dog succeeded in performing it at all and then only after some time had elapsed. On the whole it was a very pleasing performance for a first effort.

Friday 29th June

Fred and I were out together. She pointed seven rabbits in succession, which were each bowled over and then retrieved, on order, to hand. I also shot a pigeon, which she marked and retrieved to hand perfectly. I reckon she could now be said to be a useful working dog.

Sunday 5th August

Fredrika ran second to Werra in the Novice Stakes of the Scottish Field Trials Association Setter and Pointer Trial. She had two very long range points indeed and drew up on them very well. In her first run she came on point and the young dog running against her stole the point, but she backed perfectly. In the afternoon she had a point and drew on for some hundred and fifty yards or more, very steadily, before flushing a covey. I feel she has been very well worth all the trouble involved.

Postscript

My old friend David, who had been a keeper for thirty years prior to early retirement, saw Fredrika in her first days when she was still a quivering wreck and said to me in tones of amazement: 'What on earth did ye buy yon dog for?' In the years thereafter he shot over her many times and it must have been about six years later when he shot a cock pheasant which fell across the river, landed on the far side with a dropped wing, picked itself up and disappeared into some very thick gorse about a hundred yards away. 'Let's have old Fred,' he said and I duly sent her across. She swam over eagerly, though she had not seen the bird shot, then put her nose down when she reached the fall and set off at speed for the gorse. We stood on the river-bank and smoked for ten minutes or so after she had disappeared until she appeared from the gorse once again and came back at a trot with the cock pheasant firmly held in her jaws, its head well up. She swam across the river and presented it to me with justifiable pride.

David, watching the delivery to hand and sharing my satisfaction, pronounced his verdict, with which I was very willing to agree.

'There's old fail-me-never,' he announced approvingly.

The following description of a day's rough shooting might have taken place at any time during the past thirty years except that there would probably be more mention of rabbits in the bag today. This was written during the post-myxomatosis decade when rabbits were still rare in many areas and partridges at that period had suffered badly from the lethal deildrin sprays, now banned. First published in *The Roughshooter's Sport* in 1958 it is entitled 'A Very Full Day':

Dick and James are enthusiasts. They had decided on an early start and a full day's sport. So at 5 a.m. we drank our hot black coffee and loaded the shooting brake with guns, dogs and other equipment and set off for the foreshore.

151

'It's still blowing pretty hard,' commented Dick cheerfully.

'Just about blown itself out,' grunted James dourly.

It was still a very cold November night, or rather morning, and the prospects of seeing some duck were fairly good. Down at the foreshore the wind was still strong. We piled out of the car quickly and, collecting guns and paraphernalia, moved off down the familiar darkness of the high tide mark.

We had judged the time nicely and reached our pre-arranged and pre-reconnoitered positions, which we had decided on the night before, with just about a quarter of an hour to spare before first light. Already the first false dawn had begun to lighten the sky and it was once again intensely black and dark. Between gusts of wind we could hear the sound of the wildfowl on the saltings and the dogs beside us cocked their ears.

'Boom, boom.'

The sullen roar of what sounded like a double-barrelled eight-bore belonging to old Charley was carried across the estuary by the wind. For a brief instant the sound of the wildfowl in front of us was stilled, then the chattering arose again in redoubled volume accompanied by a brief stirring of wings. With the hint of first light in the sky the birds were getting restless.

While eyes strained unnecessarily, but almost inevitably against the lessening darkness there was a flicker of wings somewhere high overhead. The first of the birds in the bay were on the move. The dogs' cocked ears and moving heads gave the only clue to their whereabouts. But to have fired at them, even had they been in range, would have been to spoil the day. As the light in the east increased another wedge of duck moved over clearly audible and this time just visible.

'Boom, boom.'

Across the water the sound of Charley's eight-bore came again. Five shillings worth of cartridges, even though he loads his own, meant that he must be seeing something to shoot. Anyway this time his shots had some effect. The gathering in front of us fell quiet and then there was a movement of wings. Next moment, with the sound of many wings beating the air, like the distant stirring of a multitude, the wildfowl started to come over.

For a few minutes we were all busy. I fired both barrels at a single mallard coming over low straight towards me and was disgusted to see him fly on untouched, but I had hardly reloaded when three more came over and this time I connected satisfactorily and heard the thumps on the foreshore behind me. To my right, out of the corner of my eye, I saw James connect successfully with a high flying widgeon, sending it crumpling earthwards. From the sounds of shots, Dick on my left was also having good sport.

Finally, all too soon, it was obvious the flight was over. Turning round we set the dogs on to the task of retrieving. The bag was five mallard, three widgeon and a curlew. As that foreshore, although once excellent, is now sadly overshot, it had been as successful a day as could be expected. While we walked back we were treated to a magnificent changing colour scheme in the East. Starting from palest green the clear sky, aftermath of the night's storm, seemed to change rapidly and vividly through the entire spectrum. As we reached the car once more we all turned to look at it in silence until the rising sun, edging the horizon and tinging the sea with red, put an end to the show.

'Hm. That wasn't bad at all,' admitted James, and even he sounded slightly impressed,

'It's going to be a fine day,' announced Dick firmly.

Considerably cheered by a good start and prospects of a better day we returned to breakfast with hearty appetites eager to get on to the moor for the morning's sport. For the scheme was to go up to the hills for the morning and then down to the low ground shooting in the afternoon and possibly duck flighting in the evening, depending on how the day had gone and how we all felt about it.

We were not long in finishing our meal and getting back to the car. The dogs, equally eager to be off, were waiting determined not to be left. After a quick check, to make sure that everything needed was present, we were on our way again. Soon we were on the hill road to the moor. Up there the wind was fresh and crisp, but the sun was warm on the back and obviously the gale had just about blown itself out. The grouse on the heather called *Go-back, Go-back*, as we stopped at each gate, and we saw an encouraging number from the car. Finally we reached the clump of windblown pines we had selected as our starting point.

To our left was the isolated sheep farm. A straggling belt of bent trees behind it acted as a wind break to the huddle of granite buildings, roofed with grey slate and to the small pond in front, on which a flock of Khaki-Campbells quacked loudly. Above us the stubble of the arable fields mingled almost imperceptibly with the edges of the moor. To our right beyond the clump of trees the moor sloped down towards the burn which was the boundary.

It did not take us long to plan our campaign. The heather was thick and in quite a few places we hoped that it would still be possible to walk the grouse up over the dogs. For the rest, depending on how things worked out, we planned one or two small drives on the southern half of the moor, where the birds were likely to be sunning themselves.

As we moved across the stubbles to the edge of the moor the dogs pointed in succession two large coveys of partridges and the morning started off well with three brace of birds in the bag, before we had even reached the moor itself. In order to make our beat correctly we then had to swing right handed and down hill towards the burn. It was here that a jack snipe rising at my feet flew on to safety with a matter of six barrels discharged into thin air behind him.

Shortly afterwards a pair of blue hares ran across in front of me and, in a moment of mental aberration, perhaps unconsciously to make up for missing the snipe, I bowled them both over. As I felt the added weight in my game bag I immediately wished I had restrained myself, but it was too late by then. When the dogs came on point in front of us and a covey of grouse was flushed, well within range, I only managed to drop one bird. The others, however, performed more than adequately, each bringing down a right and left. Five more birds in the bag, but we were not to be so fortunate again.

The grouse were wary and it was a case, in the main, of snap shots with the choke barrels, but the morning passed all too quickly. Nor was it without spectacular moments, as when Dick brought down a mallard drake out of three duck flying over at an astronomical height, or when James killed an old cock grouse flying strongly at maximum range with his first barrel and then swung through ninety degrees to kill a snipe cleanly with his second. With the addition of a further hare, which seemed to be all I was able to hit, my own shooting ceased to amount of anything at all.

Fortunately there came a point when we all decided that the number of hares we had shot between us made it only sensible to form a cache of the game and return to it with the car. As a suitable track crossed the moor it was possible to do this without radically altering our plans. With the sun beating down strongly I was only too glad to leave the sweater which earlier on had seemed an essential part of the programme. In the tussocky heather there was no need to try to keep warm. Sweat was trickling down my back, where the game bag had been pressing, and my shirt was soaking, wet and clammy.

Once rid of the weight of the bag I felt I could walk on all day and I think the others felt the same. Certainly the standard of shooting improved all round and the bag mounted steadily until finally we reached the car once more. After Dick had taken the car to collect the cache we counted the total. Seven brace of grouse, three and a half brace of partridges, two brace of snipe, one mallard, eleven hares and two rabbits, with the addition of a couple of crows. Including the widgeon and the curlew shot earlier this meant nine different varieties in the bag.

'Forty-one head. A highly satisfactory morning, I call that,' said Dick cheerfully.

'It might have been worse,' agreed James, which, for him, was high praise.

We settled down with a good deal of satisfaction to a quick snack of lunch and a pipe. Conditions on the moor had proved as good as we could have wished for, with sufficient wind to carry the scent and good scenting conditions for the dogs. A touch of early morning frost, followed by unexpectedly hot sunny conditions on the moor had probably helped to counteract the birds natural wildness at this time of year, for we had certainly done far better than we had expected.

Down on the low ground we hoped to do well too, and in anticipation of good sport we did not linger over our sandwiches. Soon we were back in the car and once more opening and shutting the gates on the hill road. Then with Dick at the wheel we made good time to the old ruined castle above the river, where we had decided to start our afternoon's shooting. Here we picked up David, an old friend and retired gamekeeper, a dead shot with his old hammer gun.

'I thought we might take in the stubbles between here and that field of flowering rape, David,' I suggested. 'And then take it out slowly. What do you think?'

'There'll be good sport in that field of rape all right,' he prophesied. 'There should be a good few birds in it.'

Spreading out in line we walked up the stubbles towards the field of rape. The sun had dried out the fields and scenting conditions were not good, but the dogs pointed one covey on the way and David started off his day well with a right and left, which showed that he was in as good form as ever. It was not long, however, before we had reached the edge of the large forty acre L-shaped field of rape which had been badly laid by the gales and remained unharvested. At the base of the L was a grass bluff, dividing the field into two parts and it was here I planned to leave two guns.

'If you and James stay here, David. Dick and I will drive it to you,' I suggested.

'Right,' he approved. 'We'll soon know if the birds are there or not.'

While James and David moved into position below the bluff, Dick and I skirted the field preparatory to driving the birds towards them

'The road is the boundary,' I explained to Dick, as we prepared to start. 'Most of the birds, if they are here, will move towards the woods, there, at the top of the L, which are their home coverts. Any that break back we can take.'

Almost at once the dogs, who had been scenting busily with heads held high, came firmly on point. We approached carefully from either side and, as we did so, something like a dozen well grown pheasants rose together. Suddenly the sky seemed filled with rocketing birds going in all directions.

I swung and took a cunning old cock behind as it tried to slip craftily back towards safety, and I saw Dick swinging the other way after another bird heading for the boundary on his side. As I turned back another flew past

strongly heading in the same direction and received the second barrel. Another shot from Dick on my left indicated that he also had taken a second bird. A series of shots forward and the sight of three high birds crumpling above the bluff one after the other, proved that the others were having good sport too.

The birds we had shot were soon retrieved to hand and we started forwards again. Barely twenty yards farther on the dogs were pointing again and this time a covey of partridges rose and flew over the guns in front perfectly. Once again three birds fell.

'Better take this slowly,' suggested Dick. 'There seems to be a lot of game here.'

As it turned out that was certainly the understatement of the day, for, as we systematically cleared the base of the L, we realised that all the game for some distance round must have been feeding on that tangled and windblown flowering rape. Every third or fourth pace, it seemed, the dogs froze on another point and the guns in front were kept very busy. Several times we had both dogs out at once, each on a different runner and the sport we all had was considerable. When we finally reached the bluff and joined the others there was more picking up to be done.

'I am just about out of cartridges,' announced James in satisfied tones.

'So am I,' grinned Dick. 'The birds were there all right.' While the rest of us set about picking up the birds below the bluff, James went back for more cartridges. The first part of the field had been so successful that we were all feeling elated. By the time James had returned we had collected the game and made a cache.

'You and David go forward this time, Dick,' I proposed. 'And we'd better make it cocks only from now on, I think.'

This was agreed readily enough and when Dick and David had taken up their positions in front of the trees at the top of the L, James and I started forwards again. Suffice it to say that this drive was as successful as the first, with the birds flying very well over the tops of the trees providing some very pretty shooting. Afterwards we were all agreed that we had never seen a field so full of game without any preliminary driving.

By the time we had made sure that the last bird had been collected there was no time for more, if we were to go after duck in the evening. The light was already beginning to show signs of fading. The total bag for the afternoon was twenty-one brace of pheasants, three and a half brace of partridges, one woodcock and a pigeon, which Dick had pulled out of the heavens from pure bravado, as it sailed overhead, jinxing, and confident it was out of range.

'Will you join us at the duck, David?' I asked.

With a cheerful grin he agreed to come along and laden with full game bags, we returned to the car. Fortunately it was only a short step from there to the river bank, where we had been laying down grain for the duck, and where we were soon spaced out in semi-permanent hides. We were only just in time, for we had hardly taken up our positions before the first flight of mallard circled and then, apparently deciding all was well, volplaned down.

James's first shot in front dropped the leader and the bird behind. David's shots, sounding almost like one, immediately afterwards, brought down two more and then the remainder were jinxing and searching desperately for height, to provide Dick with one of the high shots at which he excels. The satisfactory thuds and splashes as the dead birds landed augured a good evening's flighting.

While it lasted the sport was fast and furious and, for the most part, I was occupied in setting the dogs on to those birds I thought might be in danger of being lost in the fast flowing current. With a cloudy background the birds were coming in perfectly and there was no need for decoys, even had we had time to put them out. Apart from a solitary teal and one high mallard, little came my way, but it was a pleasure to watch the others shooting. For the most part the birds fell with that decisive thump which indicates a stone dead bird and there were few shots wasted. At the final pick up we had fourteen mallard and three teal.

With the darkness now almost complete, tired, but content, we counted the total bag in the car headlights. A hundred and eighteen head in all. Counting both blue and brown hares in the morning and the crows, we had fourteen different varieties in the bag. A day that had far exceeded our most hopeful expectations. A day to remember for a long time to come. As James summed it up:

'A very full day.'

During the 1970s and 1980s and into the early '90s shooting was subject to numerous and varied pressures from many different angles. Ever more intensive farming methods led to removal of hedgerows that had provided protection for birds. Ever more lethal sprays resulted in numerous deaths of leverets, nesting birds and fledglings. The grey partridge and the brown hare became rare in areas where they had once been common. Politically there was constant pressure to ban it from the various anti-shooting groups, who also wished to ban hunting and fishing and all field sports. From certain police forces there was clamour for greater control of shotguns and after various shooting tragedies, involving maniacs with guns, it became obligatory to have a licence for all shotguns, similar to a Firearms Certificate. Whether this rendered the public any safer from criminals with hand-guns is open to question.

Further advances in game rearing making it possible for one man to rear thousands of pheasants led inevitably to commercialization of shooting on a scale never previously known. Commercial shoots, offering shooting by the week, or even by the day, became increasingly common. Shoots that had been rented by syndicates were leased instead by entrepreneurs catering for groups of friends, or businessmen.

The day of the peripatetic shooter, travelling to Scotland or Wiltshire overnight for a day's shooting before returning to London had arrived. Corporate hospitality might include such a day for a group of selected directors and their guests. Pheasants and partridges were reared in enormous numbers and inevitably not all the guns enjoying such days were good shots. Horror stories abounded of birds so badly shot that they were impossible to sell or even give away and had to be buried. Not unnaturally this sort of thing soon became the subject of considerable criticism in shooting circles where experienced sportsmen were the first to condemn such unsporting activities.

In his book *Outside Days* published in 1989, Max Hastings, editor of *The Daily Telegraph*, himself an all-round sportsman and keen shooting man, voiced in strangely familiar terms popular concern about trends current as the 1990s approached, as well as making some sound suggestions for the future. He wrote:

The greatest threat to shooting must come from the new obession with big bags and the growth of commercial shoots that seek to offer the opportunity to kill pheasants and partridges on much the same terms as a golf club offers members a round; birds are presented under rigidly controlled, artificial conditions. Any idea of wild sports or physical exertion (even by the wretched pheasants) is dispelled. There is a story of an English guest gun, invited to a French shoot. He was caught in a traffic jam on the autoroute and arrived an hour late. He was astonished to find his fellow guns still waiting patiently at the rendezvous. His host brushed aside his excuses. 'There is nothing to apologise for, m'sieur,' said the intrepid French shooter dismissively, gesturing towards a large lorry rolling up the drive. 'The birds were caught in the same jam. See, here they are now.'

A year or so ago, I was a guest at a tycoons' shoot on a 2000 acre island amid one of the North American great lakes... The line of guns walked through the woods past vast pens housing thousands of hysterical birds awaiting the call to duty. The pheasants we shot that morning had been released just an hour before. Most of the partridges were literally kicked into the air by the dog handlers, from beneath the rocks where they crouched while the pointers pointed them. Even some of the local guests declined to raise a gun to shoot them. The day was a frightening example of what field sports can become in their most corrupted form.

Game-shooting in Britain has not, mercifully, plumbed the depths that it has attained in the United States or on the Continent, with birds released from their cages, immediately before being shot. But there are strong grounds for fearing the evolving trend towards commercial shoots. These lack the sense of being a traditional part of country life, involving local people. They offer none of the uncertainty which is so important to sport, that makes the occasional blank drive...as much a part of the sporting scene as the big day...

Ten years ago it was widely agreed among British shooters that the Edwardians' enthusiasm for big bags had been incorrigibly vulgar and its absence was unregretted by their modern successors. Today, however, the age of the 'big shots' threatens to return, financed by businessmen perfectly willing to spend £10,000 or £15,000 a day to entertain their friends in a fashion they think will impress them. When the British public begins to notice what is going on, as it surely will, then all our sporting interests will be at risk. On the Continent legislation has already been passed in one country and has been threatened in several more to prohibit the shooting of birds for a specified period after their rearing and release. The pressure for similar legislation in Britain will grow, enabling those hostile to field sports to make disturbing inroads, if the new commercial shoots continue to develop along present lines.

This is especially sad when so many sportsmen are passionately devoted to the wider cause of conservation. Shooters...may justly claim that they were taking The Environment seriously long before organisations such as Greenpeace and Friends of the Earth were thought of. The Game Conservancy has a research record second to none, in studying the habitat of British wildlife and considering means by which species survival can be improved. Almost all shooters take the view that they will kill only birds and beasts that are plentiful... Statistics suggest that woodcock numbers are increasing, yet there is a growing reluctance among British sportsmen to raise a gun against these most charming of birds because of dismay at the slaughter inflicted upon them on the continent...

European abuses now pose a serious threat to British sport. There is such dismay about the reckless massacre of birds conducted by Italian, Greek and French gunmen — sportsmen seems an inappropriate description, — that there is a growing threat of intervention against *all* hunting by the EEC in Brussels. There is an important job of education to be done here by British ministers — to make Brussels understand the critical difference between the anarchistic approach to sport in some EEC countries compared with the care with which shooting and wildlife management are conducted in Britain.

The hostile publicity towards field sports generated by abuses, whether in

Britain or abroad, however, makes it all the more important that sportsmen in Britain should grant as few hostages to fortune as possible.... Many of us would like to see the field sports organisations giving a strong public lead about what sort of conduct is, and is not, acceptable... Even if BASC (The British Association for Shooting and Conservation) and BFFS (The British Field Sports Society) lack statutory powers, it would make a substantial impact on many shooters if they were formally warned that by participating in the more deplorable commercial shoots they are breaking every principle of sport, conservation and the countryside. Peer pressure can be very effective...

Masters (of hounds) and shoot captains should insist that all those who hunt or shoot with them belong to one or other field sports organisations. The Ministry of Agriculture should be explaining to the public that as farm incomes are squeezed, farmers must be allowed to earn money from field sports, if they are to be able to manage their land for the common good. Shooting will never provide a farm income substitute, but it can be a useful supplement on the margin, likely to become more popular with the introduction of 'set aside'...

In a wider sense, there is an immense job to be done, of making the public understand the direct link between field sports and conservation, in a fashion that, at present, only the Game Conservancy seriously undertakes. Very few town dwellers perceive, for instance, that it is the fact that most land and sporting rights in Britain are in private hands which ensures that our countryside and wildlife are incomparably better managed than in those parts of Europe where a free for all prevails... The future of field sports will surely hinge on how well they are seen to be conducted by the public at large, however inappropriate we may think some of the factors that influence opinion are...

Battue shooting by the start of the 1990s once again, and rightly, had become the subject of hostile criticism and since this criticism came from the foremost sporting authorities themselves, from the British Field Sports Society, from the Game Conservancy and from the British Association for Shooting and Conservation, as well as leading sportsmen, it had the effect of curbing the worst excesses.

The effects of the world recession experienced then, however, may well have done as much as anything to put a stop to this type of excessive corporate *battue* shooting. The corporations themselves could no longer afford it. With agriculture also once more in the doldrums, with land set-aside, and with rabbits recovered, more shooting was available. The grey partridge and the brown hare, both adversely affected by modern farming methods, seem to be recovering in many areas with the reduction in spraying and with more wild cover available. The costs of driven shooting might still be high, but rough shooting is once again available for those who wish it. Rather than the large driven shoot this may well be where the future lies.

It seems the wheel has turned the full circle since the days of the Georgian sportsman shooting over his dogs. But in the nature of things wheels go on turning and excessive *battue* shooting of reared birds may again become common. It is to be hoped, however, that public opinion will make itself felt and that game shooting in this country will never be allowed to decline into ignorant butchery as it has elsewhere.

An understanding of what makes anyone interested in hunting and shooting is important to anyone who wishes to take part in these sports. The first point to realize is that the distinction between the two is an artificial one introduced in Britain during the Victorian era when the rigidity of mind of the period sought to compartmentalize and label every activity. Elsewhere in the world hunting and shooting, as they used to be in Elizabethan England, are regarded as one and the same activity. When a person goes out with a gun and a dog in America, or in Europe he or she is said, rightly, to be going hunting. The following is extracted from the *Encyclopedia of Shooting:*

No doubt man first hunted for food and the true hunter's attitude to his quarry has always had an undertone of respect, of reverence, even worship, in it. Without this element there is little to distinguish man the hunter from his ancestor the ape-man. Many early cave paintings had a strong magical or religious significance and almost all early pagan religions had a close link with animals through hunting. Both Greek and Roman mythology continued the theme. The lion and the unicorn of heraldry are but one obvious instance of a modern survival of these beliefs.

The early hunter, who depended on killing his quarry to live and was constantly aware that he might himself be killed, skilfully delineated the antelope, the auroch, the bison and the mammoth among other animals on the walls of his cave dwelling. While in some cases this may simply have been a record of the hunt, in other instances he was clearly trying to establish a mystical relationship with his quarry. A belief in the resurrection of the hunter's spirit after death in the shape of the quarry he hunts is still the basis of many primitive religions. The American Plains Indian held this anthropomorphic belief in various forms well into the last century and many primitive tribes today share similar convictions.

This respect, amounting to reverence, for the quarry is to be found in the custom, not yet extinct among modern European hunters, of communing silently for a few moments beside the body of the shot stag before placing a sprig of greenery between its jaws representing its last meal on earth, or possibly as food for its journey into the next world. A twig dipped in the blood of the quarry is then placed in the hat band of the successful hunter. On a lesser scale, but with precisely similar intent, the pin feathers of a woodcock when shot are often abstracted and placed proudly in the hat band of the successful shooter. Clearly these are survivals of the earliest primitive pagan rites of man the hunter.

When the British huntsman 'bloods' the novice follower of hounds by daubing his brow with blood from the severed brush, or tail, of the fox after a successful hunt, he is unwittingly acting the part of the priest in a pagan religious ceremony. The sounding of the horn, or horns, at the successful conclusion of the hunt fulfils the twofold function of summoning the laggards, both hounds and hunt followers, as well as saluting and honouring the passing of the quarry. On the continent at the end of a shoot the game is laid out graded carefully in rows and saluted by the *Forstmeisters* with blasts on their horns in a similar manner. These are all clearly modern survivals of much older ceremonies dating back to the days of early man.

With the exception of the mating instinct the impulse to hunt is the oldest of man's natural instincts. Neither of them are anything to be ashamed of although some people, whose own instincts are often debased or atrophied beyond recognition, would have it so. In modern man, inevitably these instincts have become less keen, in some cases altered, even twisted, but this is no matter for pride.

The modern opponent of hunting or shooting generally lays claim to a civilised attitude. He implies, rightly, that he cannot understand the attitude of the hunter. He has himself generally lost the reverence for the quarry inherent in the true hunter. It would, however, be wrong simply to accuse him of lack of reverence or of atrophied instinct. It is merely understanding that he lacks. Reared from childhood on Bambi or Beatrix Potter, he often suffers from a twisted anthropomorphic belief that animals feel pain and reason like humans. Mistakenly he equates himself with hunted animals and credits them with his imaginary fear and pain. Such reasoning, of course, bears no relation to the realities of the Chase or of Nature.

It is very understandable that the modern town dweller, born and bred in unnatural concrete surroundings, knows nothing of the delicate balances of life in the wilder countryside, where Nature still holds sway. He does not appreciate that the sufferings of the lame calf striving to keep up with the herd are abruptly and mercifully stilled for ever by the jackals hovering on their trail. The game preserver who strives to understand his quarry, often becoming a first rate naturalist in the process, who admires its struggles to survive, who culls the animals which are past their prime and saves them with a merciful bullet from the defeats of old age, the rebuffs by younger animals, the final ostracism from the herd and at best a lingering death in the heavy snows of winter, is to be applauded not censured.

The opponents of hunting and shooting generally know little, and care less, about the background. They know nothing of the cold wet dawns, or long freezing evening vigils, or even of the heat and flies of summer, when any unguarded movement may betray the hunter's presence and mean many previous hours, even days, of effort and careful preparation wasted. Nor can they, generally, understand that very often it is reward enough merely to watch the quarry in its wild state, to see the delicate courtships, the fond maternal care of the mother, or the playful antics of the young.

By imbibing knowledge of every aspect of his quarry's way of life the hunter naturally increases his admiration of it. As well as a hunter he becomes inevitably a game preserver. Awareness of its courage in defence of its young, knowledge of its mating displays and ceremonial, experience of it at every season of the year, all these add up to the essential hunter's knowledge. They also add up, inevitably, to understanding, respect and even worship of a worthy adversary.

List of Sources

Alonzo Martinez de Espinar *Arte de Ballestertia y Monteria* 1644

Richard Blome *The Gentleman's Recreation* 1686

Lt. Col. Thomas Thornton *A Tour of the Highlands* 1784

Aeneas Mackintosh of Moy *Diaries* 1784

Major Hazzard *Letter from South Carolina* 1800

Lt. Col. Thomas Thornton *A Tour of France* 1802

Revd. William Barker Daniel *Rural Sports* 1801

Sportascrapiana c.1800

Colonel George Hangar *To All Sportsmen* 1812

Lt. Col. Peter Hawker *Diaries 1800–1853* and *Instructions to Young Sportsmen:*
  6th edn 1830

George Osbaldeston *Autobiography* 1786–1860

Captain Horatio Ross 1824

Charles Dickens *The Pickwick Papers* 1840

Strathconan Estate Records 1841

Sir Samuel White Baker *With Rifle & Hound in Ceylon* 1852

J. S. Walsh *Manual of Rural Sports 'Stonehenge'* 1856

Charles St. John *Wild Sports of the Highlands* 1846

James Forsyth *The Highlands of Central India* 1871

Thomas Speedy *Sports in the Highlands & Lowlands* 1874

William Bromley Davenport *Sport* 1884

Charles Lancaster *The Art of Shooting* 1889

Chauncey Hugh Stigand *Hunting the Elephant* 1913

James Sutherland *Adventures of an Elephant Hunter* 1912

Sir Peter Mackie *The Keeper's Book* 1913

T. H. White *England Have My Bones* 1935

Michael Bratby *Grey Goose* 1939

Julian Tennyson *Roughshooting* 1938

Michael Brander *The Roughshooter's Sport* 1958

Michael Brander Ed; *The Encyclopedia of Shooting* 1972

Max Hastings *Outside Days* 1988

Acknowledgements

The author and publishers are grateful to the following for permission to use copyright material in this book: David Higham Associates and William Collins for the extract from *England Have My Bones* by T. H. White; Michael Joseph Ltd, and Max Hastings for the extract from *Outside Days* © Max Hastings 1988; A. & C. Black (Publishers) Ltd, for the extract from *Rough Shooting* by Julian Tennyson. Every effort has been made to contact copyright owners but in some instances this has not been possible.